Discrete Trial Training

A Tribute to Rich Simpson

Dr. Richard L. Simpson unexpectedly passed away just as this series was about to go to press. He had a significant and profound impact on each of us, the field of special education, and the areas of autism and behavior disorders in particular. Dr. Simpson spent 42 years of his career at the University of Kansas, from where he led the field in developing teacher preparation programs for future educators of students with autism and behavior disorders. He also conducted research to identify scientifically validated practices, and published over 200 articles, books, and book chapters. His work guided the field's effort to bridge the gap between research and practice and advanced the movement to identify and use evidence-based practices that improved the lives of children and youth with autism and their families. Many revered Dr. Simpson. His numerous awards and public recognitions reflect a distinguished career of considerable contribution.

Dr. Simpson was also a remarkable and inspiring teacher and mentor. His knowledge was awe-inspiring, yet he was approachable and personable. He supported graduate students by providing them with many opportunities to publish and conduct research and to complete professional presentations and school-based consultations. His students will carry his legacy throughout the world, working as teachers, school administrators, consultants, researchers, and professors, all serving children and youth with autism and their families.

Those who knew Dr. Simpson will remember his friendly and caring disposition, great sense of humor, and quick wit. He was a wonderful friend to many, and his guidance and encouragement were unparalleled. He will be missed by many, in ways that are too numerous to count.

PRO-ED Series on Autism Spectrum Disorders
Second Edition

Edited by Richard L. Simpson

Titles in the Series

Visual Supports—Second Edition
Discrete Trial Training—Second Edition
Naturalistic and Incidental Teaching—Second Edition
Social Skills and Social Interactions—Second Edition
Assistive and Instructional Technology
Sexuality Education
Self-Management and Cognitive Behavior Interventions
Functional Behavioral Assessment
Self-Determination

PRO-ED Series on Autism Spectrum Disorders
Second Edition

Discrete Trial Training
Second Edition

Sonja R. de Boer

pro·ed
An International Publisher

800-897-3202   Fax 800-397-7633
www.proedinc.com

© 2018, 2007 by PRO-ED, Inc.
1301 W. 25th St., Suite 300
Austin, Texas 78705-4248
800-897-3202   Fax 800-397-7633
www.proedinc.com

Library of Congress Cataloging-in-Publication Data
Names: DeBoer, Sonja R., author.
Title: Discrete trial training / Sonja R. de Boer.
Other titles: How to do discrete trial training
Description: Second Edition. | Austin, Texas: PRO-ED, Inc., [2018] | Series:
    PRO-ED series on Autism Spectrum Disorders | Previous edition published:
    Austin, Texas : PRO-ED, Inc., [2007] | Includes bibliographical references.
Identifiers: LCCN 2017053086 (print) | LCCN 2018014745 (ebook) |
ISBN 9781416411413 (pdf) | ISBN 9781416411406 (paperback)
Subjects: LCSH: Autistic children—Education. | Autistic children—
Behavior modification. | Learning.
Classification: LCC LC4717 (ebook) | LCC LC4717 .D43 2018 (print) |
DDC 371.94—dc23
LC record available at https://lccn.loc.gov/2017053086

Art Director: Jason Crosier
Designer: Lissa Hattersley
This book is designed in Nexus Serif TF and Formata Sans.

Printed in the United States of America

2 3 4 5 6 7 8 9 10 11   30 29 28 27 26 25 24 23 22 21

Contents

From the Editor

Children and youth with autism spectrum disorder (ASD) routinely demonstrate exceptionally demanding and distinctive characteristics and needs. Even when compared to other disabilities, ASD is especially complex and perplexing. Learners diagnosed with ASD exhibit a range of social interests and cognitive and communicative abilities; and they commonly display a variety of challenging behaviors. Still, many children and adolescents with ASD have normal patterns of growth and development, a wide range of distinctive assets and capabilities, and highly developed and inimitable abilities. These widely varied and unique features necessitate specially designed interventions and strategies orchestrated by knowledgeable professionals. When supported by the right combination of well-informed professionals (and in many instances, parents and family members) and appropriate methods and intervention strategies, children and youth with ASD show significant progress. Without a doubt, consistent and correct use of effective methods, as presented in the current series, is the key to achieving successful outcomes with individuals with ASD.

Preface to the Series

Identification, correct implementation, and ongoing evaluation of scientifically supported practices are essential features of effective programming for learners with ASD. Unquestionably, there is a clear-cut link between the use of interventions and supports with empirical backing and positive school and postschool outcomes. Different terms, including *evidence-based procedures and practices, scientifically supported interventions*, and *research-validated methods*, all refer to methods and practices that have been successful in bringing about desired changes based on objective and empirically valid research. Unfortunately, practitioners all too often fail to use these proven tools and procedures, or use them the wrong way.

Indeed, this research-to-practice gap is a major obstacle in efficiently and effectively addressing the needs of learners with ASD and creating optimal pathways to the best outcomes. This is not a problem of motivation, intent, or objective. Educators and other professionals, as well as parents, families, and other stakeholders, want the most effective methods and updated ASD information. Regrettably, clearly written, practitioner- and family-friendly materials that provide straightforward information are in short supply.

This concern was the motivation for creating the current resources. Each book in the series provides utilitarian, down-to-earth information on using an intervention or support method, with potential to produce significant benefit. Each of the 10 books, written in a user-friendly and straightforward fashion by experienced, internationally recognized professionals, offers practical information, solutions, and strategies for successfully supporting individuals with ASD and related disabilities.

Several of the books focus on using applied behavior analysis (ABA), the single most verified intervention tool for learners with ASD.

- de Boer provides step-by-step guidance on using discrete trial instruction and related methodology.
- Tincani, Lorah, and Dowdy direct readers in how to design maximally effective management programs via functional behavior assessment and analysis.

Other skill-development foci are covered in the series, each with an emphasis on the practical application of documented methods.

- Stichter and Conroy address the ever-pressing issue of building social skill assets among children and youth with ASD and harnessing the support of peers.
- Charlop provides a practitioner-friendly explanation of naturalistic teaching strategies and incidental teaching methods.
- Ayres and Whiteside provide essential information on how to take advantage of assistive and instructional technology tools to teach and support learners with ASD.
- Earles-Vollrath, Cook, and Kemper describe in detail efficacious visual supports that can help children and youth with ASD function more independently.
- Crutchfield and Wood provide readers with clear-cut instruction in the use of cognitive behavior modification, self-management, and self-monitoring methods.
- Shogren and Wehmeyer, via their book on self-determination, offer specific and clearly described strategies for ensuring that individuals with ASD are fully and deservedly involved in their program plans and outcomes.
- Finally, Travers addresses the all-too-often-neglected topic of sexuality among adolescents and young adults with autism-related disabilities.

Richard L. Simpson
Series Editor

Acknowledgments

My love and appreciation to my mom, Suzanne de Boer, and to my husband, Kai Schraml, for all their support and editing and being great sounding boards as I ramble on about ABA and DTT! I also sincerely thank Richard Simpson, who has always been an amazing editor and colleague and has the patience of a saint!

Appendix K uses symbols from Mayer-Johnson:
> The Picture Communication Symbols ©1981–2015 by Mayer-Johnson LLC, a Tobii Dynavox company. All Rights Reserved Worldwide. Used with permission.

Boardmaker® is a trademark of Mayer-Johnson LLC.
> Tobii Dynavox
> 2100 Wharton Street, Suite 400
> Pittsburgh, PA 15203
> Phone: (800) 588-4548
> Fax: (866) 585-6260
> E-mail: mayer-johnson.usa@mayer-johnson.com
> Web site: www.mayer-johnson.com

⚙ Introduction

To be able to use the discrete trial training (DTT) method with students with autism spectrum disorders (ASD), the reader first needs to have an understanding of the disability itself. The brief description that follows will ensure that all who read this manual understand the definition of ASD and the foundation it provides for the use of DTT.

In May 2013, the fifth edition of the *Diagnostic and Statistical Manual of Mental Disorders* (DSM-V) was officially sanctioned for use by the American Psychiatric Association (APA; 2013). One of the major changes in the new edition was a complete revision of the diagnostic criteria for ASD. The Asperger Syndrome diagnostic classification was eliminated, along with other specific subtypes of autism, and replaced with a continuum of severity. Individuals with severe forms of autism fall at Level 3, moderate is Level 2, and mild forms are coded as Level 1.

The Autism Spectrum Disorder Diagnostic Criteria of the DSM-V (APA, 2013) outline five factors that professionals should utilize to determine whether an individual manifests an ASD; a table delineates the three dimensions of severity in which an individual would be classified. In summary, the diagnosis considers social communication and social interaction deficits; restricted and repetitive behaviors or interests; symptoms evident at an early age; symptoms resulting in significant impairment in current functioning; and symptoms that cannot be otherwise explained by other disabling conditions, specifically, cognitive impairments. For each of the two deficit areas of social communication and social interaction and restricted and repetitive behaviors or interests, the three classifications of severity essentially fall within the levels of mild (requiring support), moderate (requiring substantial support), and severe (requiring very substantial support).

It is important to note that many professionals, families, persons with autism, and persons previously identified as having Asperger's Syndrome do not agree with this new diagnostic criteria. No matter the type and amount of disagreement, the important thing is that individuals with ASD receive appropriate and intensive intervention. The most scientifically proven and supported methods are based on applied behavior analysis (ABA).

One common characteristic among all individuals with ASD, no matter the severity of their diagnosis, is their unbalanced pattern of skill development (Burack & Volkmar, 1992; National Research Council, 2001; Van Meter, Fein, Morris, Waterhouse, & Allen, 1997). For instance, an individual with ASD may display math skills several years beyond his age yet may be unable to use the toilet independently. In this connection, individuals who teach and plan skill development programs for learners with ASD, including professionals and parents, typically consider the following skill domains: (a) cognition, (b) learning, (c) social interaction, (d) play, (e) communication, (f) adaptive behavior, (g) behavior, (h) motor, and (i) sensory sensitivities (Atwood, 1998; Koegel, Koegel, Frea, & Smith, 1995; Mauk, Reber, & Batshaw, 1997; Myles & Simpson, 2003). Related to these domains, this manual provides information on teaching skills to children and youth with ASD via the DTT method.

To assist readers in understanding and using the DTT method, the following information is provided:

- a brief description of ABA as it relates to DTT and ASD;
- a brief description of the antecedent, behavior, and consequence paradigm;
- a description of the concepts imbedded in the structure of the DTT paradigm;
- a list and description of teaching concepts and skills needed to provide a structured teaching environment for using DTT with students with ASD;
- a brief description of how to assess the needs of a student and set up an effective teaching program;
- a brief description of the data-based decision-making process that is needed in a DTT program;
- a description of the procedures for evaluating the performance of instructors implementing DTT programs with students with ASD;
- a set of evaluation/observation forms to be used with new instructors;
- other forms, diagrams, procedure sheets, and data sheets; and
- a glossary of terms.

Examples and practice exercises are also provided throughout the book to help readers gain guided practice and a firm understanding of the concepts and skills that form the foundation for DTT.

1 Applied Behavior Analysis as It Relates to Autism Spectrum Disorder and Discrete Trial Training

Applied behavior analysis (ABA) is the process of systematically applying the principles of behavior to "improve socially significant behavior to a meaningful degree and to demonstrate experimentally" that the procedures used were actually responsible for the change (improvement) in the behavior (Cooper, Heron, & Heward, 1987, p. 14). Accordingly, an instructor *applies* behavior principles in order to change an individual's *behavior* and then *analyzes* whether the actions taken caused a behavior to change. A crucial component of ABA is the process of *improving the social significance* of the individual's behavior. That is, it is important that the change in behavior be observable, meaningful, and important; such changes might include learning to read, add and subtract numbers, not hit other people, follow a teacher's instructions, or engage in a conversation with another person. For a change in behavior to be socially signifi-cant, the individual must also demonstrate *independence* and *generalization* with the skills and behaviors he has learned. If a student participates in an inten-sive ABA educational and behavioral intervention program for 25–40 hours a week but cannot perform any skills independently in different environments in which he needs to use those skills, that ABA program has not been a successful intervention program and has not benefited him. The old myths regarding ABA that came about during the early days of research with ABA and children with autism spectrum disorder (ASD), alleging ABA only creates little robots, need to be continually challenged and shown to be false. This process is achieved when learners with ASD who receive ABA interventions and supports are trained in flexible and dynamic environments for independence and generalization.

A significant amount of scientifically based research on ABA has been con-ducted (starting in the 1960s), and no other intervention method has proven more effective with individuals with ASD (Simpson et al., 2004). Studies have demonstrated that using ABA intervention methods with individuals with ASD can produce comprehensive and lasting improvements in many important skill areas, including language, academics, behavior, and social interaction. Behav-ior analysts view ASD as a "syndrome of behavioral deficits and excesses that have a neurological basis but are nonetheless amenable to change in response to specific, carefully programmed, constructive interactions within the environment" (Green, 1996, pp. 29–30).

For over 2 decades there have been calls for the use of evidence-based and scientifically supported methods with children and youth with ASD and other disabilities. In 2001, the U.S. Department of Education's Office of Special Education Programs requested that the National Research Council (NRC; a part of the National Academy of Science) establish the Committee on Education Interventions for Children with Autism to investigate and "integrate the scientific, theoretical, and policy literature and create a framework for evaluating the scientific evidence concerning the effects and features of educational interventions for young children with autism (ages 0–8)" (NRC, 2001, p. 2). In 2001, the NRC published a book titled *Educating Children with Autism* in which it recommended that "educational services [for children with autism] begin as soon as a child is suspected of having an autistic spectrum disorder" and "those services should include a minimum of 25 hours a week, 12 months a year, in which the child is engaged in systematically planned, and developmentally appropriate, educational activities aimed toward identified objectives" (p. 2). It is critical to recognize that *early and intensive intervention* is the most important aspect of the research in regard to the treatment of individuals with ASD (Matson & Jang, 2013; NRC, 2001; Smith, 2001). The second most important factor in early intervention for individuals with ASD is that the intervention be based on the principles of ABA (Matson & Jang, 2013; NRC, 2001; Smith, 2001).

In 2013, Matson and Jang published an article in which they comprehensively reviewed published studies using evidence-based ABA intervention methods with children with ASD. The studies had to be intensive (over 20 hours of intervention per week), had to provide 1:1 staff-to-student ratio services, and had to be comprehensive intervention programs that addressed all aspects of autism (communication, adaptive skills, academic, self-help, behavior, etc.). They found a total of 21 studies (published from 1998 to 2012). All the studies applied ABA evidence-based methods and used the following methods and procedures: (a) discrete trial training, (b) modeling/imitation, (c) prompting, (d) reinforcement (primary and secondary), (e) fading, and (f) shaping (Matson & Jang, 2013). In sum, these ABA-supported interventions were the most effective means of achieving socially valid outcomes with children and youth.

Most recently, in 2015, Leaf et al. (all pioneers in the field of ABA) identified the four main components of effective early intensive behavior intervention (EIBI):

- hours of treatment/intensity (sometimes referred to as dosage) at 25–40 hours per week;
- a comprehensive approach that includes language development, social skills, self-help skills, academics, play, and leisure skills;

- highly trained staff implementing the program with a focus on treatment integrity (fidelity of implementation); and
- ABA training received by staff specific to population being served.

In another recent study, Dixon et al. (2016) examined how a student's learning (mastery of specific skills and behavior objectives) aligned with the skill and training of program supervisors. Variables considered were (a) supervision hours for each student/case, (b) credentials, (c) years of experience, and (d) caseload (638 students/cases were included in the study). Two of these elements were found to have a significant impact on student learning and mastery of skills. First, those students with ASD who had a Board Certified Behavior Analyst (BCBA) supervising their program mastered significantly more learning objectives. Specifically, "supervisors with BCBA certifications produced 73.7% greater mastery of learning objectives per [treatment] hour as compared to supervisors without a BCBA" (Dixon et al., 2016, p. 345). Second, a program supervisor's years of experience showed a significant impact on student learning. Specifically, the study revealed that "for every year of experience that a supervisor had, the number of mastered learning objectives increased by 4%. This may be trivial when considering the impact of a single year, but would indicate that cases [students] that are supervised by practitioners with 10 years of supervisory experience are mastering 40% more per [treatment] hour." (Dixon et al., 2016, p. 345)

In summary, ABA intervention methods offer families and professionals an evidence-based and systematic process for teaching skills in a way that allows individuals with ASD to most efficiently and effectively understand and learn. Discrete trial training (DTT) has been determined to be one of the most effective ways of using ABA to teach children and youth with ASD. But it is imperative that ABA intervention programs for children with ASD, including DTT, involve highly trained and competent professionals. Research supports that these are behavior analysts who hold BCBA certification.

2 The Antecedent, Behavior, and Consequence Paradigm

The antecedent, behavior, and consequence (ABC) paradigm (Cooper et al., 1987) is a fundamental concept within ABA and DTT. All ABA procedures involve the manipulation of one or more components of this three-term contingency plan (see Table 1).

The ABC paradigm allows analysis of behavior that is occurring in *any* environment. By recording the occurrence of a behavior and the events that occurred immediately before and after the behavior, one is able to evaluate the cause (antecedent) and effect (consequence) of a behavior. By using a data collection system to maintain a record of the behavior, along with the antecedents and consequences of each occurrence, one is able to track and analyze patterns that occur and thus more accurately instruct a learner in a new skill and otherwise intervene to increase or decrease the occurrence of the behavior. The following are examples of the ABC paradigm:

Reinforcement of Appropriate Behavior
A: Adult is holding a cookie within view of a child.
B: Child asks adult, "Cookie, please?"
C: Adult gives the child the cookie.

Reinforcement of Inappropriate Behavior
A: Adult is holding a cookie within view of a child.
B: Child throws a tantrum and tries to take cookie from adult.
C: Adult gives the child the cookie.

Table 1. Antecedent, Behavior, and Consequence Paradigm

A Antecedent	B Behavior	C Consequence
The stimulus under which a behavior occurs	An action that occurs in response to an antecedent	A response that follows a behavior that will either increase or decrease that behavior

These two examples include the same antecedent and the same consequence, but the child displays and is reinforced for different behaviors. In the first example, the child asks for the cookie appropriately, and the adult gives it to him; in the second, the child inappropriately throws a tantrum and tries to take the cookie from the adult, and the adult gives it to him. An instructor can view these data and see that in the future, the first child will most likely continue to appropriately ask for things that he wants, and the second child will continue to try to grab things from people or throw a tantrum when he wants something.

Important information can be gained by using the ABC paradigm to analyze behaviors. ABC data are very useful in revealing why a behavior occurs and in what situations it is most likely to occur again. These data can also reveal what consequences are causing a behavior to increase or decrease and, therefore, help instructors determine appropriate consequences to use in the future.

3 Using the Discrete Trial Method to Teach Skills

Understanding the structure and use of the three-part ABC paradigm is essential to understanding and using DTT and maximizing an individual's learning. This method of teaching involves the following:

- breaking a skill into smaller parts,
- teaching each part to mastery,
- providing concentrated teaching,
- providing prompting and fading as necessary, and
- using reinforcement procedures.

Each DTT teaching session involves a number of trials, each of which has a distinct beginning and end, hence the term *discrete*. The DTT method is distinguishable from traditional teaching methods because it prescribes presenting a very small unit of information and immediately seeking the student's response. Active instructor and student involvement is an element of DTT.

The DTT method mirrors the ABC paradigm as follows (see Table 2). Just as the ABC paradigm is used to analyze a behavior that a student is demonstrating, the DTT method is a more narrowly focused paradigm for analyzing the learning behavior of a student. Each DTT element is recorded: the instruction provided (antecedent), the student's response (behavior), and the instructor's response to the student (consequence). This basic DTT process enables one to evaluate the cause (antecedent) and effect (consequence) of a student's learning. Using a data collection system that assists in maintaining a record of a student's responses to specific instructions and the consequences that follow those responses, an instructor can track and analyze the effects of instruction (and specific materials)

Table 2. The Discrete Trial Training Method:
A Mirror of the Antecedent, Behavior, and Consequence Paradigm

S^D Discriminative stimulus	R Response	S^R Consequence
The instruction, question, or relevant materials presented to the student (the antecedent)	The student's reaction to the S^D (the behavior)	The reaction provided by the instructor to the student in response to the student's behavior (the consequence)

7

and consequences and thus ultimately increase or decrease the occurrence of specific responses of the student with greater accuracy. Three examples of different ways, both appropriate and inappropriate, to increase or decrease the occurrence of a specific response follow. In these examples the discriminative stimulus is represented by S^D, the student's response is represented by R, and the instructor's response, or consequence, is represented by S^R.

Reinforcement of Appropriate Response (increases response)

S^D: Instructor says, "Give me sock." (A sock is lying on the floor in front of the student.)

  R: Student picks up the sock and hands it to the instructor.

S^R: Instructor says, "All right! Good job" and tickles the student, who laughs in response.

No Reinforcement of Inappropriate Response (decreases response)

S^D: Instructor says, "Give me sock."

  R: Student looks around the room and does nothing.

S^R: Instructor says, "Let's try again."

Reinforcement of Inappropriate Response (increases response)

S^D: Instructor says, "Give me sock."

  R: Student looks around the room and does nothing.

S^R: Instructor says, "Come on, Johnny. Here is the sock—see it?" and tickles the student, who laughs in response.

The first example presents an instructor appropriately reinforcing a student for a correct response. Accordingly, in the future, the student is more likely to correctly identify a sock. The second example presents an instructor appropriately not reinforcing the student's failure to respond to the instruction. Therefore, the instructor has decreased the likelihood of the student not responding in the future. The third example presents an instructor *in*appropriately reinforcing the student for not responding to the instruction. Even though the student did not respond correctly to the instruction, the instructor reinforced him. Therefore, in the future, the student is more likely not to respond to an instruction because he has learned that he may still receive reinforcement.

There are two important reasons to use DTT with students with ASD. First, because students with ASD do not naturally gain information from their environment by observing and listening to others or modeling others' behavior, the DTT method enables instructors to systematically analyze tasks that a student needs to learn, break them down into small, defined steps, and systematically teach them to a student in incremental elements that she can more easily learn.

This method also enables different teachers to be consistent in their instruction by clearly writing out the procedures for implementing a discrete trial (S^D–R–S^R). This strategy supports teaching consistency—in instructional language, presentation of the S^D, and application of consequences—thereby facilitating student learning. It also allows instructors to more easily and more accurately collect data, because the trial is clearly and simply defined and easily recognized.

For each component of the discrete trial, there are important factors to remember that will enable an instructor to more successfully teach students with ASD, as discussed in the following sections.

Delivery of Instruction: Discriminative Stimulus

Delivery of the discriminative stimulus (S^D; instruction) involves several critical steps. First, it should be presented in a simple, straightforward, and concise manner to ensure student understanding. Thus, for instance, a teacher's instruction to a student might be "Find circle" rather than "Can you find where the circle is?" This allows the student to hear only the two most important words—she is supposed to *find* something, and that something is a *circle*. Extraneous language can confuse the student or cause her to attend more to the other words or lose her attention altogether. Later, when attempting to help the student generalize her skills, the teacher should add more words to the instructional commands and statements.

Second, all instructors need to be consistent in the way they present the S^D, including how they present stimulus materials, the language they use, and so forth. This is especially important during the initial teaching phase of each skill. Later, as the student advances with his skills, instructors need to add words to the instructional phrase, add different instructional phrases and sentences, and otherwise present commands and directions in a fashion that is more typical of routine instruction.

Third, only when the student is paying attention and motivated to respond should the instructor provide an S^D. This step is an important and crucial part of the student's learning and is foundational for the success of future learning. If students fail to learn to attend to someone who is speaking to them, they will have significant difficulty acquiring skills. It is a skill that will be displayed differently by each student. It does not necessarily include maintaining eye contact with the instructor. Attending means that the student is ready to receive the S^D and is motivated to provide a response. A student shows that she is ready when she

- is not preoccupied with any other activity, object, or person; and
- is stationary in the appropriate location designated by the instructor.

It is evident that a student is motivated when she indicates that she wants to obtain a specific reinforcer that the instructor has made available contingent on a correct response. Teachers must continuously evaluate the effect of the reinforcers they are using to find out what the student wants and, therefore, what will help motivate the student to respond to the S^D and acquire skills.

While it is most desirable for a student to attend by looking directly at the instructor when he is providing an S^D, this should not be expected initially or required because of the difficulty that students with ASD often display in acquiring that skill. It is not realistic to believe that, by forcing a student to look at the instructor's face or eyes, the student can be made to attend to the instructor. An instructor can help the student learn how to be ready for instruction by taking a known tangible reinforcer, bringing it up in front of his own face to direct the student's eyes toward his face, and simultaneously orienting the student toward the source of instruction and reinforcement. It also is beneficial for the first S^D of a session or series of trials to require an easy or already acquired response—something the student knows and will be successful with. Beginning a session on a successful note will often help to ensure that the student will attend to future S^Ds.

Fourth, the instructor should present an S^D only once. Only if it is apparent that the student did not hear the instructor, or was not attending, should the instructor provide the S^D again. If a student is accustomed to an instructor providing an instruction an indeterminate number of times, the student will learn that he may respond whenever he wants to. This can lead to difficulties with compliance with other instructors, as well as difficulty with learning appropriate social interaction skills. For example, if a typical peer has to ask the student a question more than two times, the peer may lose interest in pursuing further interaction. If the student learns that the instructor will provide the instruction only once, and if no response is provided no reinforcement will be received (the instructor instead commences with the correction procedure, which will be discussed later), the student is more likely to learn to respond the first time an instruction is provided.

Fifth, the student's name should not be used within the S^D. It may seem beneficial to use a student's name (e.g., "Johnny, give me sock") because it is a way of obtaining the student's attention. Yet there are a couple of possible adverse effects that may hinder the student's future learning. First, by using a student's name, the instructor may inadvertently teach the student that she needs to pay attention only when her name is used in the S^D. Therefore, even when she is the only one present with the instructor and the instructor says, "Give me sock," the student may not respond. Second, if a student hears her name within each S^D throughout the day, her name may become aversive. She may run away or purposely not attend to the instructor when she hears her name, because she has learned to associate an instruction with it.

Present instruction

- in a *concise* manner,
- *consistently* across all instructors,
- only when the student is *attending* and *motivated*,
- only *once*, and
- *without* using the student's name.

Obtaining the Correct Response

The second part of the DTT method, response (R), is composed of three elements that are connected to a student's ability to provide a correct response. First, it is important for all instructors to agree upon and consistently use correct response criteria. An example of two instructors accepting different responses follows:

- Instructor 1 says, "Where is your nose?" Student points in the general direction of his nose without actually touching it.
- Instructor 2 says, "Where is your nose?" Student actually touches his nose.

Adverse effects can result if different instructors accept different responses from a student as being correct. The student may become confused and give a different response to each instructor each time he is asked to respond to an S^D. Inconsistent standards may result in students learning different sets of skills for different instructors and responding in a certain way based on who is providing the S^D.

Second, instructors need to ensure that the response a student provides is not chained to another response. It is important that a student provide only one response to an S^D. When a student is unsure of what response to provide, she may attempt many different responses in the hope that one of them is correct. An example follows:

S^D: Instructor says "Show me jumping."
R: Student pats head, waves, jumps up and down.

If the instructor reinforces the student after she has provided the correct response along with other responses, the student may learn that all three behaviors are "jumping" and will then be confused when she is requested to "show waving" or "show patting head."

Third, the instructor needs to wait approximately 1–7 seconds after the S^D is delivered for the student to provide her response. It is important for the student to have enough time to recall the correct response, while also maintaining attention to the task at hand. The amount of delay time between the S^D and the response will vary for different students and skills. Accordingly, instructors need to collaborate to decide on an acceptable delay time. The following four components need to be considered in this decision.

1. *Difficulty of the task.* Typically, the more difficult the task, the longer the delay between the S^D and the response. Often, an instructor can see that a student is thinking and attempting to recall the correct response. As long as the student appears to be thinking or problem solving, the instructor should wait for the student.

2. *Fluency.* This refers to how quickly and accurately a student can provide a correct response. Fluency is not expected when a student is acquiring a new skill. Also, each time a new skill is introduced into the same category of acquired skills (e.g., within the *food* category, a student is provided novel food items in addition to the ones he already knows), it will affect the fluency of production of the already acquired skills.

3. *Determination of time needed to respond.* Some instructors use "rapid responding," wherein they require students to respond within 1 second after receiving an S^D; if a student does not do so, the instructor immediately prompts him to provide the correct response. Rapid responding may be appropriate for some students when working on fluency of acquired skills but not for skill acquisition. Adjustment of response time should be based on whether students are working on new skills or an acquired skill. After working with a particular student, instructors should be able to see a pattern in that student's learning habits. Based on that analysis, instructors should be able to accurately determine approximately how long they should wait for a response when teaching a new skill or attempting to generalize acquired skills.

4. *Avoidance of prompt dependency.* A student becomes prompt-dependent when she consistently waits for an instructor's prompt before providing a correct response. Prompt dependency may result under the following conditions:

   - Students with ASD may become upset when they fail at a task, so they figure out ways to ensure that they do not fail and look for any type of prompt, subtle or obvious, to point to the correct response.
   - Instructors provide prompts that are not systematically faded quickly enough.
   - Subtle prompts (which the instructor did not intend to provide) are consistently provided along with the S^D and not faded. For example, when asking a student to pick the red item in a display of green, blue, and red blocks, the instructor's eyes look at the red stimulus.

- Students with ASD are unmotivated to respond and learn that, when they don't respond correctly (or don't respond at all), they are assisted in making the correct response.

It is imperative that instructors and those who supervise instructors of students with ASD have a carefully developed protocol related to the prompts and prompting methods that will be used. Prompting and fading methods are discussed later.

☆ Quick Review: Obtaining the Correct Response

- Know the correct response expected.
- Ensure that the response is *not chained* to another response.
- When waiting (1–7 seconds) for the correct response, take into consideration the following:
  - difficulty of the task,
  - fluency,
  - response time,
  - prompt dependency, and
  - acquisition of new skill versus generalization of acquired skill.

Providing Immediate Consequences

The third part of the DTT method involves consequences for students' responses. In this connection two matters are particularly important. First, an instructor needs to provide feedback (consequences) to the student after she provides a response to an S^D. Because students with ASD have difficulty learning, it is crucial that the instructor present the appropriate consequence immediately following the response. Here is an example of an instructor providing inappropriate feedback (consequences):

S^D: Instructor says, "Show me clapping."

R: Student claps her hands appropriately.

S^R: Instructor rummages through a box next to her looking for a specific toy to give to the student as a reinforcer for making the correct response; several seconds later she hands the toy to the student and says, "Good clapping."

In the meantime, the student sat and watched another student play with a music toy and then looked out the window. When she finally receives the toy and hears "Good clapping," she may not remember that she just did clapping or may not pay attention to the "Good clapping" and think she got the toy for appropriate sitting. Providing *immediate* reinforcement for a correct response will increase the likelihood that the correct response will occur the next time the same S^D is provided. Here is an example of an instructor providing appropriate feedback (consequences):

S^D: Instructor says, "Show me clapping."

R: Student claps her hands appropriately.

S^R: Instructor immediately says, "Good clapping" and hands the student a ball.

Second, it is important for instructors not to *inadvertently* reinforce an incorrect response. Instructors may not realize that they are accepting a response as correct when other instructors are not accepting it. For instance, some instructors may say, "Good job" before they proceed with a correction procedure because they want to reinforce the student for trying to provide the correct response. By saying that, however, they may be communicating to a student that an incorrect response was correct. As previously indicated, some instructors may also reinforce a student for providing a correct response within a chain of other responses. It is essential that all instructors provide clear and consistent reinforcement and feedback. If a student provides an incorrect response, the instructor's immediate response should be to initiate a correction procedure that teaches the student the correct response. If a student's response is correct, the immediate result should be reinforcement that further strengthens the behavior.

☆ **Quick Review: Providing Immediate Consequences**

Remember to

- provide immediate reinforcement for a correct response, and
- avoid inadvertent reinforcement of an incorrect response.

Utilizing Inter-Trial Intervals

The last component of an actual "trial" is the inter-trial interval. It is the time and space between the occurrences of one trial of S^D–R–S^R and the next trial of S^D–R–S^R. It signifies to the student that a trial has ended. It also gives some time for the consequences that the instructor provided to essentially sink in with the learner and finalize the learning sequence that took place in the trial. This time should be short and last for only about 3–5 seconds (Malott & Trojan-Suarez, 2004). If too much time elapses, the instructor may lose the behavioral momentum already achieved, which is another important factor in delivering discrete trials (see the section on behavioral momentum).

Often the inter-trial interval (often abbreviated as ItI) is not formally written on any procedure sheet or DTT protocol script. It is something that the instructor must be trained to do; it is then assumed the ItI will always naturally occur when instructors use discrete trials with a student. During this time the student should not be playing or engaging in self-stimulation (aka stimming) with the materials.

If the student responded correctly to the instruction that just occurred, the student may engage with the reinforcer the instructor provided for him. If the student responded incorrectly, then he would need to wait appropriately for the next trial to begin (i.e., with quiet mouth and hands down). For some students, sitting/waiting appropriately may actually be a prerequisite skill (one of the crucial learning-to-learn skills) that needs to be taught prior to engaging in the teaching of academic or play skills.

The instructor would typically use those few seconds to record the data from the trial just completed and, if needed, change the teaching materials that are in front of the student. At the end of the ItI, the instructor would end the student's time playing with the reinforcer, if applicable, and ensure that she has the student's attention in order to give the S^D that begins the next trial.

This may sound like a lot of different tasks that the instructor needs to accomplish and think about during the ItI, but they quickly become unconscious and natural skills that one does not think about anymore when implementing DTT to teach a student new skills. Also, it is important to distinguish between the time interval between trials that occur within a set of trials being used to teach a specific skill in that moment (e.g., 5–10 mass trials) and the time interval that occurs between the instructor's finishing one set of trials and starting a new set of trials about a different topic (e.g., working on colors and then working on numbers). This between-task time interval may be longer than the intervals during the set of trials when a skill is being taught. In these situations, the child will typically stay at the desk (or be allowed a quick break away from the desk) but can be engaged in different activities.

☆ Quick Review: Utilizing Inter-Trial Intervals

At the end of each discrete trial, remember to

- allow 3–5 seconds between each trial to signify to the student that the trial has ended,
- keep the ItI as short as possible so behavioral momentum is not lost,
- ensure that the student is behaving appropriately during the ItI, and
- use the time to record data and change out any teaching materials.

Summary

The discrete trial teaching method to teach students with ASD can be viewed as both complicated and simple. It can appear complicated because there are many steps to remember when using it to teach a student new skills. Yet, in reality, it is a simple and straightforward instructional method.

The basic discrete trial method consists of three major components: (a) the instructor provides a simple instruction (S^D), (b) the student provides a response (R), and (c) the instructor provides a consequence to the student's response (S^R). The overall and more complete discrete trial actually comprises five components:

1. The instructor provides a simple instruction (S^D).
2. A prompt is provided as needed. (This is explained thoroughly in the prompting and fading section.)
3. The student provides a response (R).
4. The instructor provides a consequence to the student's response (S^R).
5. There is a 3–5 second ItI.

It is beneficial to spend time practicing the DTT method with coworkers before using it with children and youth with ASD. This ensures that practitioners are comfortable and consistent with the process and that they have an opportunity to provide feedback to one another and to sharpen their skills before using DTT with students. Table 3 can be used by teams of instructors to structure their practice. It includes columns for recording appropriate S^D phrases, correct student responses, and appropriate consequences.

Once instructors become adept with the basic skills involved in using DTT, they need to understand other crucial aspects of using DTT with students with ASD. The next chapter discusses those components, which will help instructors to provide the structure that students with ASD need to successfully learn and generalize new skills.

Table 3. The Structure Used to Practice Discrete Trial Training

S^D Discriminative stimulus	R Response	S^R Consequence
Instructor says, "Give me pencil."	Student picks up and hands instructor the pencil.	Instructor says, "Great, Michael—this is pencil!"
Instructor holds up a child's book and says, "Where is the dog?"	Student points to the dog in the picture.	Instructor says, "Yeah! You found the dog! Good work!"
Instructor and student are standing in front of a sink and instructor says, "Wash your hands."	Student picks up the soap and starts playing with it.	Instructor takes the soap, puts it down, and says, "Let's try again."

4 Providing a Structured Teaching Environment for Skill Acquisition

A structured teaching environment is vital for the successful use of the DTT method. The following concepts, methods, and procedures are important for instructors to employ:

- errorless learning,
- task analysis,
- reinforcement,
- pairing,
- instructional control,
- behavioral momentum,
- session management,
- prompting and fading,
- shaping,
- chaining,
- error correction procedure,
- transfer trials,
- token economy systems, and
- discrimination training.

The following sections provide an overview of each of these teaching concepts, methods, and procedures. Each section contains the following:

- a definition (also provided in the glossary),
- a detailed explanation of the concept and implementation of the necessary procedures,
- examples of using the procedures with students with ASD,
- a "Practice Beginning Exercise" and/or "Practice Role-Play Scenario" for practicing the procedure, and
- a "Quick Review" of the important concepts regarding that procedure.

One important aspect of implementing DTT is ensuring that it is utilized appropriately with students and implemented as it was designed to be—that is, with treatment integrity or fidelity of implementation (Babel, Martin, Fazzio, Arnal, & Thomson, 2008; Belfiore, Fritts, & Herman, 2008; Bolton & Mayer, 2008; Dixon et al., 2016; Leaf et al., 2015). This means that all new instructors need to be consistently and constantly evaluated on their performance with DTT until they are deemed competent. The process for appropriate performance evaluation is discussed in a later chapter. Observation forms to be used for practice and evaluation of the procedures described throughout this book are provided in the appendices.

Errorless Learning

Errorless learning involves teaching a new skill in a manner that minimizes the possibility of errors and thus increases the possibility that the student will be a successful learner. Errorless learning

- minimizes the number of errors a student will make,
- increases the time available to the instructor to engage in teaching rather than correcting the student,
- reduces the likelihood that errors will be repeated in the future, and
- reduces a student's frustration and inappropriate behaviors by increasing opportunities for the student to be reinforced for correct responses.

Everyone has memories of having difficulty learning a new skill. For all learners, including those with ASD, there are typically three reasons why they cannot successfully acquire a skill:

- they do not have the abilities required to perform the skill,
- they do not have the desire to learn the skill, or
- they are not appropriately taught how to perform the skill.

If instructors ensure that they are correctly and appropriately teaching skills to students with ASD, they can then concentrate on whether the students have the ability to acquire and perform the skill and are motivated to learn the skill. Thus, errorless learning is a teaching method by which instructors ensure that they are helping students successfully learn a skill if the students are motivated and capable.

A practical example of errorless learning can be found in sports. Athletes on a sports team routinely learn new skills and work to improve acquired skills. Their coaches are responsible for teaching them the skills they need to compete. When a new player joins a team, the coach typically does not expect that individual to already have all the skills she needs to compete and be a successful and proficient team member. When coaches teach their athletes a new skill, they must:

- ensure that the athletes are motivated to learn,
- break the skill into smaller steps,
- explain the function and use of the skill,
- demonstrate the skill,

- provide prompts needed to perform the skill initially,
- shape performance of the skill,
- provide immediate and relevant feedback regarding performance of the skill, and
- require that the athletes practice the new skill so that they become fluent in its execution and can use it at any appropriate time or place.

If coaches merely tell athletes to perform a skill that they have not yet acquired and have no prior knowledge of, they will begin the learning process by making mistakes. Those mistakes may hinder the athletes from being successful in the future and increase their frustration, thereby decreasing their motivation to learn the skill. This same pattern applies to teaching students with ASD. The two most important times during the DTT process to use errorless learning with a student are

- each time a new skill is taught, and
- when a student is demonstrating difficulty with an acquired skill.

An instructor needs to break each new skill into small, acquirable steps; model and otherwise demonstrate the skill; and then initially provide a high level of prompting, thereby ensuring motivation while decreasing frustration and increasing the likelihood that a student will be able to provide a correct response. This will increase the probability that the student will be successful in the future, as the instructor begins to fade the prompts. The process of fading will be discussed in a later section.

When a student is demonstrating difficulty with learning a new skill or is consistently demonstrating incorrect responses for a previously acquired skill, an instructor needs to immediately stop requiring independent responses. The instructor should begin a process of "backing up" in order to diagnose the learning difficulty and find out where the student is able to provide an independent successful response. Once this is achieved, the instructor employs the errorless learning approach and begins by breaking down a given skill into small steps, demonstrating the skill, and providing a high level of prompting when presenting the S^D. Providing a high level of prompting along with an S^D is an integral part of the errorless learning process. This allows the instructor to

- maintain the student's motivation, while decreasing his frustration; and
- increase the likelihood of future correct answers.

☆ Quick Review: Errorless Learning

Using errorless learning helps to

- minimize the number of errors a student displays,
- reduce the likelihood that errors will be repeated,

- reduce the student's level of frustration and the occurrence of inappropriate behaviors,
- increase time available to teach, and
- increase opportunities for reinforcement of correct responses.

Remember to

- use this approach when teaching a new skill or helping a student who is having difficulty with an acquired skill,
- present an S^D with enough of a prompt to ensure a correct answer, and
- provide a high level of reinforcement for a prompted correct response.

Task Analysis

At the beginning of the previous chapter, as well as in the section on errorless learning, "breaking a skill into smaller parts" was listed as one of the basic and essential strategies for implementing DTT. Breaking a skill down into individual steps involves task analysis. This process may at first be difficult, because a typical learner does not usually think about or see all the small individual steps that he goes through in learning to do a task, such as learning about the category of animals, what they are, what sounds they make, and so on. After a person gains experience, task analysis becomes easier, and anyone can pick a task to analyze and teach to a student in the home, community, or school. When it comes to teaching skills to children with ASD, the task analysis process is preferably led by the supervisor (i.e., ideally a BCBA) of a student's overall ABA program.

A brief description of what task analysis is and why it is important is provided so that the reader can understand how and why it is an essential part of the DTT process. In the chapter "Assessing Students and Establishing an Overall DTT Program" (near the end of the book), more detailed explanations and examples are given for developing procedure sheets for teaching a specific skill to a student. The task analysis process described below is what is used to make or understand already developed procedure sheets for instructors to use and follow in teaching skills.

Task analysis is a component of errorless learning because it allows an instructor to know how to errorlessly teach a skill. The result of a task analysis will give an instructor the sequence of steps to follow to lead a student to learn a particular skill. Overall, there are three task analysis procedures:

1. forward chaining (i.e., teaching a skill in sequence, beginning with the first steps and moving forward)
2. backward chaining (i.e., teaching a skill in reverse sequence, beginning with the final steps and moving backward)

3. whole task presentation (i.e., teaching a skill that one needs to generalize and use in many different contexts, such as identifying colors or
numbers)

Chaining involves completing several skills in a specific sequence in order
to complete an overall task, such as washing hands or tying shoes. (As a teaching
tool, chaining is discussed in a later section, which includes further explanations
and examples.)

Before one approaches a skill to do a task analysis, three things need to be
done:

1. Define the target skill/behavior.
2. Collect data on the current occurrence of the behavior; this is the
baseline data process.
3. Write out a clear goal for the student to achieve to demonstrate mastery in learning that skill/behavior.

Once this process has been completed, the instructor can analyze the skill/
behavior to be taught. First, the instructor needs to determine if the student has
the prerequisite skills to learn the new target skill. If not, these skills need to be
taught first and are essentially the beginning of the sequence of steps in the overall task analysis. Second, the instructor needs to watch someone perform the skill
or perform the skill herself to determine all the smaller sequential components
of the skill. As the instructor watches or performs the skill, she needs to write
down the steps that are taken, in the correct sequence. The first time an instructor completes a task analysis for a specific skill/behavior, it is important that she
then ask a couple of people to follow the exact sequence of steps that she has listed
to determine if a step has been omitted and if the people reach the planned end
result. The instructor also needs to clearly describe and create (if needed) the materials that will be used when teaching the skill.

The overall task analysis should result in a set of steps that are:

- discrete (isolated and distinct from each other),
- manageable and logical for the student to perform once he has learned
the previous step, and
- clearly described so that every instructor teaches the skill the same way
and knows what to expect the student to do (S^D, R, and S^R are defined for
each step).

☆ Practice Exercise

Choose two people to work together and have them pick a typical skill that would
be taught to a student with ASD. Before engaging in further discussion, each

person should break down the skill into smaller steps and write them down in the order that they would be learned and performed. The two people should then compare their lists and think through what they did and did not consider when completing their individual task analysis. They can also answer questions, such as (a) did they use the same definition of the skill/behavior? (b) did they establish a clear goal so that they had in mind what the end result of the skill or behavior looked like? (c) did they remember all the important steps and make sure each was a logical and manageable next step for the student to perform? (d) and so forth. Appendix A provides a task analysis checklist to use during and/or after the process to evaluate a person's performance.

☆ Quick Review: Task Analysis

To complete a successful task analysis, remember to do the following before teaching a skill to a student:

- clearly define the target skill;
- collect data on the current state of the target skill;
- set achievable goal(s) for the student to acquire the skill;
- break down the target skill into a sequence of smaller manageable steps;
- ensure that each step is discrete and logically follows the previous step;
- have other instructors review, practice, and refine the sequence of steps; and
- prepare all the materials that will be needed.

Reinforcement

The assertion that a student needs to be motivated in order to learn is well documented. When using the DTT process, instructors employ reinforcement and prompting to motivate students to learn. (Prompting is explained in detail in a later section.) *Reinforcement* involves providing a consequence following a student's response that increases the likelihood that the response (behavior) will occur again in the future. A reinforcer is anything that the student wants to gain (e.g., food, attention, toys). Food and drink are primary reinforcers because they are biological and something that all humans need and want (though how much and how often may vary). Other reinforcers, such as praise, a toy, or tokens, are secondary reinforcers; they require conditioning in order to be reinforcing. In other words, secondary reinforcers need a positive history of association with primary reinforcers in order to make them reinforcing in and of themselves, because they may initially not have any reinforcing value. Thus, when working with young children with ASD and/or working with students with ASD who are new to learning through DTT, instructors need to determine if they need to start with primary reinforcers during teaching sessions before slowly teaching the value of secondary reinforcers. Teaching the value of secondary reinforcers can be very effectively done through the use of token economy systems. (Procedures for creating and implementing token economy systems are discussed in a later section.)

It is important for instructors to understand that any behavior or response—inappropriate (incorrect) or appropriate (correct)—can be reinforced. It is, therefore, important for instructors to closely monitor the type of consequences that follow a student's responses. Four examples are provided to demonstrate appropriate use or withholding of reinforcement and inappropriate use or withholding of reinforcement. Some of these examples are similar to previous examples provided:

Reinforcement of Appropriate Behavior
A: Adult is holding a cookie within view of a child.
B: Child asks adult, "Cookie, please?"
C: Adult gives the child the cookie and says, "Good asking."

No Reinforcement of Inappropriate Behavior
A: Adult is holding a cookie within view of a child.
B: Child throws a tantrum and tries to take the cookie from the adult.
C: Adult ignores the child, walks away, and hides the cookie.

Reinforcement of Inappropriate Behavior
A: Adult is holding a cookie within view of a child.
B: Child throws a tantrum and tries to take the cookie from the adult.
C: Adult gives the child the cookie.

No Reinforcement of Appropriate Behavior
A: Adult is holding a cookie within view of a child.
B: Child asks adult, "Cookie, please?"
C: Adult ignores the child and does not give the child the cookie.

The first and second examples illustrate an instructor who is *appropriately reinforcing* a student for a correct response and not reinforcing a student for an incorrect response. This instructor is appropriately using reinforcement to increase appropriate responses or behaviors and decrease inappropriate responses or behaviors. The third and fourth examples present an instructor who is *inappropriately reinforcing* a student for an incorrect response and not reinforcing a student for a correct response. This instructor is inappropriately using reinforcement and will likely increase inappropriate responses or behaviors and decrease appropriate responses or behaviors.

There are two primary purposes for using reinforcement during the DTT process. First, reinforcement is a critical factor in teaching a student new skills. By tying reinforcers directly to the target behavior that the instructor wishes to increase, the student is taught the correct response. Second, reinforcers can provide the motivation a student needs to learn a skill that he may not necessarily care about or whose importance he does not understand. A student needs to see a reason (a "payoff") for providing a response, specifically a correct response, to an S^D. If the instructor makes it clear that he has something the student wants to obtain, the student will be more apt to be motivated to do what the instructor requests in order to obtain that item or activity (the reinforcer).

It is imperative that instructors use reinforcers that the *student* prefers and not reinforcers that the *instructor* chooses and thinks the student prefers. Consistently employing the use of a reinforcer assessment (a checklist of items and activities the student has preferred in the past and novel, age-appropriate items the student may prefer) will allow an instructor to find out what the student wants to gain and will provide ideas for new items and activities that the student may like. Because the strength of a reinforcer (the amount of motivation that the reinforcer elicits) can vary from moment to moment, instructors need to implement a quick reinforcement survey at the beginning of each learning session. This will ensure that the student is highly motivated and decrease the likelihood of incorrect responses resulting from lack of motivation. When possible, it is appropriate and beneficial to allow the student to choose (prior to a learning session) what he would like to earn as a reinforcer after successfully completing a particular learning session (a larger reinforcer than what is earned at intervals during the learning session). Choice, in and of itself, can be a motivating factor that leads to successful learning, as it can make a student feel that he has some control over his environment and his learning. For example, an instructor knows that a particular student enjoys looking at books, playing on the computer, and playing with trains, so he pulls out a choice board with some pictures on it when he and the student sit down to begin working together. One picture shows a student working appropriately with an instructor, and there is an arrow to a blank spot. There are three pictures at the bottom of the board of the student reading books, playing on the computer, and playing with trains. The instructor asks the student to pick what activity he would like to do after "doing good work." The student picks a picture and puts it next to the arrow, establishing his choice to play with trains when they finish working. The board remains visible throughout the session.

There are four crucial factors that an instructor needs to take into consideration regarding the use of reinforcers. First, in order for a reinforcer to be effective it needs to reinforce the actual skill or behavior that is appropriate and desirable or that the instructor is trying to teach. Effective reinforcement means that a reinforcer is provided to the student *immediately* after the appropriate behavior or correct target response occurs. There cannot be a long space of time, nor can other skills or behaviors be performed/demonstrated in between the occurrence of the target skill/behavior and the delivery of reinforcement. This may sound logical and simple, but once this is pointed out to instructors, many are surprised at how often they inadvertently provide reinforcement to a student after he or she has engaged in other behaviors after performing the target behavior. This often happens with self-stimulation (i.e., stimming). For example, during a session, there is a discrete trial in which a student correctly identifies the blue ball and then starts flicking his fingers in front of his eyes, and then the instructor hands him a piece of a cookie, saying "Good job! That's the blue ball." In this scenario, the student was just reinforced for engaging in the self-stimulation behavior of flicking his hands in front of his eyes, a behavior that the instructor does not want to reinforce and increase.

Second, there should be reinforcers that the student has access to only during learning sessions and not during the rest of the day, either at home or at school. This ensures that the reinforcers maintain their strength and that the student does not become satiated. These items may be kept in special containers in locations that the student cannot access. Special reinforcers may also be used for some specific, very difficult learning activities. For example, if a student loves M&Ms and particularly dislikes writing activities, a teacher might provide one whole M&M to the student for every word she writes without protesting. Those candies would not be used during other learning sessions.

Third, the amount or level of reinforcement provided to the student needs to match the level of difficulty or desirability of the task he is being asked to perform. This is called differential reinforcement. If the student enjoys the task or the task is fairly easy for the student, he requires smaller amounts of reinforcement or reinforcement at less frequent intervals. If the student dislikes the task or the task is difficult, he will likely need a larger amount of reinforcement or reinforcement at more frequent intervals. Instructors need to pay attention to the amount of motivation that the student displays to perform various tasks and should provide enough reinforcement to ensure that the student maintains a high enough level of motivation to perform a particular task. Generally speaking, difficult tasks need more reinforcement and easy tasks need less reinforcement. High motivation needs low reinforcement; low motivation needs high reinforcement.

Fourth, the student should be provided access to reinforcers *only* when she has earned them. That is, to receive a reinforcer, a student must comply with a request or respond correctly to an instruction. Inappropriate behavior, noncompliance, and incorrect responses do not earn reinforcement. For the student to learn, she must understand that she must do or give something in exchange for something that she wants.

There are two different schedules of reinforcement that instructors use when teaching students: continuous reinforcement and intermittent reinforcement. Continuous reinforcement means reinforcing the student every time he performs the correct skill or behavior. Intermittent reinforcement means that the student is reinforced for performing the correct skill or behavior only sometimes. Continuous reinforcement is used when teaching a new skill. Every time the student responds correctly, the instructor reinforces her because the instructor wants her to know that that response/behavior is correct and to do it again in the same way the next time. After a while, however, the student may become satiated (have all that she wants) if she is reinforced every time she performs the skill. A student's motivation to continue to perform a skill typically decreases if the same thing happens over and over. But if she doesn't know when she will be reinforced for responding correctly, then she will typically try harder and be more motivated to continue to provide the correct response with the hope that *this* time she will get that reinforcer; this is intermittent reinforcement. Therefore, as a skill becomes acquired, the instructor will decrease the frequency of reinforcement in order to maintain the motivation to continue to perform that skill and to perform it correctly. There are different kinds of intermittent reinforcement that the reader may want to investigate further. Some of these strategies involve detailed and complicated formulas of fixed and variable ratios of reinforcement (after a designated amount of times the skill is performed correctly) and fixed and variable intervals of reinforcement (after a designated amount of time has passed with correct skill performance occurring during that time). However, DTT practitioners are often able to formulate their own individual reinforcement schedules for individual students.

If these DTT-related reinforcement methods are not learned and followed by instructors, their ability to teach students with ASD will be impeded. Thus, the process of a student learning a skill is the responsibility not only of the student but of the teacher as well. If a student is not learning a particular skill, instructors need to analyze whether reinforcement is being appropriately employed. They must ask the following questions:

- Is the student being provided access to reinforcers as a consequence of making correct responses?
- Does the student want to gain the reinforcer that is being offered?
- Is the student being provided reinforcement only when he provides a correct answer?
- Does the amount of reinforcement match the difficulty or preference level of the task?
- Is the student showing signs of satiation with the reinforcers?
- Is the instructor providing immediate reinforcement for the correct response, or possibly inadvertently reinforcing other behaviors or skills?

☆ Practice Role-Play Scenario

Have two people work together as an instructor and a student, or have an instructor work with a real student with ASD. Pick a skill to work on while a third person observes and analyzes how the instructor assesses what the student finds reinforcing and how the instructor uses the different aspects of reinforcement with the student during the teaching session. Review the results together. Appendix B provides a reinforcement evaluation/observation form.

☆ Quick Review: Reinforcement

Remember to

- use items and activities that are highly preferred by the student as reinforcers,
- provide access to reinforcers only when the student has earned them and only in small amounts,
- allow access to specific reinforcers only during work sessions,
- provide reinforcement immediately after the correct response,
- determine if continuous or intermittent reinforcement is needed to maintain the student's motivation to continue to respond correctly,
- make sure that the amount or level of reinforcement matches the level of difficulty or desirability of the task,
- consistently perform reinforcer assessments in order to keep a current record of the student's likes and dislikes, and
- gradually increase expectations of correct responses for the same level of reinforcement.

Pairing

Pairing is a process whereby the instructor establishes herself as a reinforcer by associating herself with other, already existing reinforcers. That is, she pairs herself with items and activities that the student already prefers and thus establishes herself as a reinforcer. She becomes a person the student wants to be with, rather than a person the student tries to get away from or is unmotivated to be near. Pairing is important because it establishes a foundation upon which an instructor can build to teach students skills they need to learn. If students like to be with their instructors, they will be more motivated to do what is requested of them.

Most students with ASD have previously worked with at least one instructor, and sometimes many. As a result, these students frequently have a presumption of what to expect from instructors, and their expectation may be good or bad, affecting their desire to learn positively or negatively. Establishing rapport with a student will directly affect an instructor's ability to teach and the student's willingness to learn. If appropriate pairing has correctly taken place, the student will be more apt to view the instructor as a "giver of good things," which will positively affect the student's learning.

There are two critical steps that an instructor takes to pair with a student. First, the instructor identifies items and activities that the student prefers and consistently seeks. The instructor then plays with those items with the student or engages in those activities with the student, as in the following examples:

- If the student likes to play with musical books, the instructor sits with the student and reads a book with him, and together they push the buttons to activate the music.
- If the student likes to swing, the instructor goes outside with the student and pushes him on a swing and talks and laughs with him.

Such sharing begins the pairing, or bonding, process. After several times of engaging in play with the instructor using such items and activities, the student will be more inclined to want to be with the instructor.

Second, as much as possible, instructors need to avoid associating themselves with negative events. For example, if a student has been playing alone with a preferred item or activity, an instructor should briefly play with the student in the presence of or using the preferred item or activity before transitioning her to a less preferred activity. This will ensure that the student does not associate the instructor with the removal of preferred items or activities.

The following are reminders of things that are important for the instructor to do when pairing with a student:

- offer access to reinforcers that the student cannot access independently (can obtain only through the instructor);
- offer access to reinforcers in small amounts to increase the frequency of interaction with the student;
- gradually increase the demands placed on the student to gain the reinforcer; and
- pair frequently with the student, not just when first getting to know or starting to work with the student.

The following are reminders of things that are important for the instructor *not* to do when pairing with a student:

- do not interrupt the student while she is engaging in a reinforcing activity (unless it is time to end the activity);
- do not turn reinforcement into a task;
- do not place demands on the student when initially pairing with her; and

- if a student gains access to a reinforcer when she should not have it, do not attempt to grab it away; instead, distract the student and then discreetly remove it or ask for it (see the discussion of the "give it back" routine in the instructional control section).

To maintain rapport with a student, an instructor needs to be mindful of pairing

- when first beginning to get to know and work with the student,
- at the beginning of every work session,
- throughout the work sessions, and
- outside of work times.

It is important for the instructor to make time to simply play with the student and not work. This allows the student to view the instructor as fun to be with independent of work.

An instructor must constantly evaluate herself to make sure she has appropriately paired with a student. One key factor to consider is whether the student runs *to* or *away from* the instructor. It is also important for the instructor to evaluate whether she looks forward to or avoids working with the student. Teaching should be as enjoyable for the instructor as learning should be for the student.

Pairing with a student also presents an opportune time to conduct reinforcer assessments, in which the effectiveness and strength of reinforcers are evaluated (ideally, frequently). During such times, new items and activities can be introduced to the student to ascertain his interest in them. A record of those the student consistently likes and does not like can be maintained as a part of his record.

☆ Practice Role-Play Scenario

Have two people play together as an instructor and a student, or have an instructor play with (or next to) a real student with ASD. A third person observes and analyzes how the instructor pairs with the student throughout the play session. Review the results together. Appendix C provides a pairing evaluation/observation form.

☆ Quick Review: Pairing

Remember to

- pair yourself with existing reinforcers to establish and maintain rapport with the student,
- avoid associating yourself with negative events, and
- reevaluate continually to make sure pairing is effective.

Instructional Control

Instructional control refers to the instructor's creating a high probability of evoking a correct response. Establishing instructional control involves understanding the sequence of events that prepares a student to respond appropriately to and learn from an instructor. It also prepares the instructor to successfully teach the student. By pairing oneself with reinforcers that motivate the student to give correct responses, an instructor can establish a successful learning pattern for the student and thereby increase instructional control.

The two critical elements involved in establishing instructional control are the association of the instructor with the delivery of reinforcement (pairing) and having students provide correct responses subsequent to receiving the S^D. These elements are independent of one another, but if either one is not occurring, the instructor will be unable to establish instructional control.

Both of these elements relate to the instructor pairing process. Once an instructor and a student have successfully paired and the student views the instructor as a reinforcer, the instructor can establish student compliance with the instructions (S^Ds). The instructor gradually increases the demands placed on the student in order for the student to gain instructor reinforcement. Initially, every instruction provided by the instructor will be reinforced by the instructor, thus strengthening the likelihood that the student will comply with (provide a correct response to) the next instruction. At first, the instructor will want to provide easy requests and instructions for the student to follow so that the student's motivation to comply will be high when task difficulty is increased. Thus, as instructional control is being established, compliance is primarily being worked on. Gradually, as the strength of the instructional control is increased, the frequency of reinforcement is decreased and the difficulty of the tasks is increased.

One particular skill to be worked on during the process of establishing instructional control is having the student give an item to the instructor when it is requested or stop an activity when told to do so. The goal is to teach the student to believe "Every time I give something to the instructor, I will get it back soon" or "Every time I have to stop doing something, I will be able to do it again soon." The instructor is establishing a relationship that is based on trust—students give items to the instructor because they know that if they give them to the instructor right away, they will get them back. Therefore, even though a student may not want to give a preferred item to an instructor or stop a preferred activity, she will do it upon the instructor's request because there is the much more preferred payoff of getting the item back or being able to do the activity again. If there is an item or activity that the student consistently refuses to give back or stop doing, that item or activity will likely be an unsatisfactory reinforcer because it inhibits, rather than increases, a student's learning success.

During the times that instructors are pairing with students, they can engage in "give it back" or "stop and do it again" routines. Initially, instructors may engage in parallel play with toys or activities that are similar to those that the student is playing with or engaged in. Playing next to the student will show the student that this particular adult is not threatening; his presence does not mean that preferred items will be taken away or preferred activities have to stop. Once the student displays consistent acceptance with this routine, the instructor attempts to briefly, and at varying intervals, interact with the student by touching the item with which the student is playing and saying something about it or otherwise attempting to briefly become part of the activity in which the student is engaging. This routine continues until the student displays tolerance.

Next, the instructor finds a moment when the student's hands are not on the item (or are not clutching the item), picks it up, does one brief action with it, and then either puts it back down or hands it to the student. That is, for a moment, the instructor interrupts the student's activity and then allows it to continue. This routine continues, and the intervals and lengths of interruption increase—but the interruptions occur because the instructor is becoming a part of the activity in which the student is engaged, not because he is making the student do work on a specific skill. The instructor can make up games with the student in which they take turns with the item or engage in the activity (the words "my turn" and "your turn" can be used). Once the student displays consistent tolerance for this type of playing, it is appropriate to begin requesting the item directly or asking the student to stop an activity ("Give me" or "Come here" or "Time to stop"). It is important that the instructor take the item or have the student stop the activity for only a few seconds and then give it back or let the student immediately resume playing. This continues to show the student that she will be able to play with the preferred item or engage in the activity again. Eventually, the instructor uses this skill during work sessions, so that there is not a struggle or display of noncompliance when he asks the student to complete a work session.

As noted in the pairing discussion, it is important to *maintain* instructional control. Instructional control is established over time. Accordingly, instructors need to continue to work at instructional control so that compliance with requests and instructions is maintained. The following methods are useful for maintaining instructional control and are similar to those used in pairing:

- **Instructors must provide only small amounts of reinforcement**; this maintains the strength of the reinforcer, which in turn increases the possibility of obtaining a correct response to an S^D.
- **Instructors need to maintain control of the reinforcers**; access to reinforcement is only through the instructor. This increases the interactions the instructor will have with students and, therefore, potentially

increases positive interactions with them, which causes them to view instructors as reinforcers.

- **Instructors must avoid presenting S^Ds that compete with any existing reinforcement**; competing with a reinforcer for the student's attention decreases instructional control. If the student already has the reinforcement that she wants, she will not be motivated to attend to or comply with the instructor's request, thus decreasing instructional control. This is why it is important for the instructor to obtain compliance with a request for an item or for cessation of an activity in which the student is engaged.
- **Instructors need to increase the number and difficulty of tasks gradually over time**; more should eventually be required for the same amount of reinforcement. Increasing the difficulty of tasks leads to the student gaining the ability to function more independently and typically within her environment. Also, if a student is not consistently challenged, she will be less motivated to attend to instruction or provide correct responses.

☆ Practice Role-Play Scenario

Have two people work together as an instructor and a student, or have an instructor work with a real student with ASD. Pick a skill to work on while a third person observes and analyzes how the instructor establishes and maintains instructional control with the student during the session. Review the results together. Appendix D provides an instructional control evaluation/observation form.

☆ Quick Review: Instructional Control

To establish instructional control,

- pair yourself with reinforcement that motivates the student,
- place the contingency of reinforcement on compliance to instruction,
- provide easy requests at first,
- decrease the frequency and level of reinforcement and increase the difficulty of task as instructional control is increased,
- establish trust by returning items taken or returning to activities that were stopped,
- maintain control of reinforcers,
- present instructions that do not compete with reinforcers, and
- increase the number and difficulty of tasks.

Behavioral Momentum

Behavioral momentum is a concept and method used in ABA when teaching new behaviors and skills. Learning something new is always more difficult than performing already mastered skills. In this connection behavior analysts draw on theory from physics: Once something is already moving, it is easier to keep it moving.

Behavioral momentum basically means building up momentum relative to what an instructor wants a student to do. This involves gradually building energy and force toward achieving a goal (i.e., by tossing out easy or "throwaway" demands) that learners will likely be successful in doing. Or to put it another way, student learning initially focuses on what students are interested in and successful in doing rather than what the *instructor* ultimately wants them to learn and be able to do.

In DTT, behavioral momentum is used as an antecedent management or proactive strategy for increasing the likelihood that the student will respond appropriately to an instruction to do something that is at a higher level of difficulty. This is particularly applicable to learning new tasks or acquiring new skills, which are universally more difficult than using established skills. The goal is to decrease the likelihood of students demonstrating challenging behaviors to escape the demands of performing difficult or new tasks and responding appropriately and correctly. Thus, the instructor first presents the student with several easy and mastered tasks at a high pace before presenting a more difficult task. By providing praise and small amounts of reinforcement for the easier, previously learned tasks, and by helping the student be successful several times in a row in performing an established behavior, the instructor is increasing the likelihood that the student will be amenable to performing a more difficult task. High levels of reinforcement are provided contingent upon students complying with and correctly responding to the instructions to perform the more difficult task.

As previously discussed in the section on reinforcement, this higher level of reinforcement for completing a more difficult task is both a teaching tool ("Yes! That is correct!") and a way of motivating the student to perform more difficult tasks in the future (i.e., because he gains more reinforcement). It is important to keep in mind that what is "easy" or "difficult" for a particular student is always changing and relative to his current skill level. Instructions for easy tasks should be simple and brief. They should also involve use of familiar instructions/tasks that have been successfully completed in the past. By following a pattern of easy-easy-easy-hard-easy-easy-hard, the instructor increases the student's motivation to engage because the instructor is building in many opportunities for success. Motivation and compliance are crucial components of skill acquisition; when they are lacking, learning is impeded. Using behavioral momentum not only boosts motivation and compliance, it also gives the student the confidence she needs to complete tasks and shapes her overall success with skill performance and compliance with instructions in general.

The main components of behavioral momentum are as follows:

- Present 3–5 easy and mastered tasks for the student to perform at the beginning of a teaching session to build behavioral momentum.
- Provide praise or very small amounts of tangible reinforcement after each correct response for the easy tasks.
- Present the easy tasks at a quick pace so that the student's attending and responding are maintained.
- Ensure that three consecutive correct responses for easy tasks are provided before presenting the difficult tasks.
- *Always* provide a higher amount of reinforcement for the more difficult tasks than for the easier tasks.
- Intersperse easy and difficult tasks throughout the whole teaching session to maintain behavioral momentum.

The following are examples of building, maintaining, and reestablishing behavioral momentum during DTT sessions.

☆ Building Behavioral Momentum at the Beginning of the Session

Presentation of "easy" tasks:

S^D: "Touch your nose." (R: student touches nose);
S^R: "Great!";
S^D: "Stomp your feet." (R: student stomps feet);
S^R: "Awesome!" (tickles student's tummy for 1 second; student wiggles and giggles);
S^D: "Wave your hands." (R: student waves hands);
S^R: "Yeah! Good work!";
S^D: "Point to the red card." (R: student points to the red card);
S^R: "Good! That's red!"

First presentation of "difficult" task (no extra time between presentation of last "easy" task and first presentation of "difficult" task):

S^D: "What does a cow say?" (R: student says, "Mooooo.");
S^R: "Yeah! Here is a cookie for you!" (gives student a cookie as a high-level reinforcer for the correct response to the more difficult task).

☆ Maintaining Behavioral Momentum During the Session
(continuation of the above example)

Presentation of more "easy" tasks:

S^D: "Where is the dog?" (R: student points to picture of dog on the desk);
S^R: "Great!";
S^D: "Show me jumping." (R: student stands up and jumps a few times, then sits down);
S^R: "Good jumping!"

Presentation of "difficult" tasks:

S^D: "What does a cat say?" (R: student says, "Meooow.");
S^R: "Yes! A cat says meow!" (gives student a piece of a cookie);
S^D: "What does a cow say?" (R: student says, "Mooooo.");
S^R: "Yeah! You are so smart!" (tickles student, while handing student a whole cookie).

Presentation of more "easy" tasks:

S^D: "Point to the bunny." (R: student points to picture of bunny on the desk);
S^R: "Nice job!";
S^D: "Where is your nose?" (R: student points to nose);
S^R: "That's right!"

Presentation of "difficult" tasks:

S^D: "What does a dog say?" (R: student says, "Ruff-ruff.");
S^R: "Good job!" (hands student a piece of a cookie);
S^D: "What does a cat say?" (R: student says, "Meooow.");
S^R: "That's great!" (hands student a piece of a cookie);
S^D: "What does a cow say?" (R: student says, "Mooooo.");
S^R: "Yeah! A cow says, 'Moooo!'" (tickles student, while handing student a whole cookie).

End of Session

☆ Reestablishing Behavioral Momentum After Losing It

Middle of teaching session—presentation of "difficult" tasks following success with previous "easy" tasks:

S^D: "What does a dog say?" (R: student says, "Ruff-ruff.");
S^R: "Good job!" (gives student a piece of a cookie);
S^D: "What does a cat say?" (R: student says, "Ruff-ruff.");
S^R: "Let's try again!";
S^D: "What does a cat say?" (R: student says, "Ruff-ruff" while looking out the window);
S^R: "Nope."

S^D: "Clap your hands." (R: student claps hands);
S^R: "That's right."
S^D: "Touch your ear." (R: student touches ear);
S^R: "Good.";
S^D: (with prompt) "What does a cat say? Meow." (R: student says, "Meooow.");
S^R: "That's right."
S^D: "What does a cat say?" (R: student says, "Meooow.");
S^R: "Yeah!" (tickles student).

Presentation of additional "easy" tasks after regaining behavioral momentum:

S^D: "Touch your head." (R: student touches head);
S^R: "Nice job!"
S^D: "Do this." (instructor waves hands in air above head); (R: student waves hands in air above head);
S^R: "That's right!"
S^D: "Stomp your feet." (R: student stomps feet);
S^R: "Good work!"
S^D: "Point to the bunny." (R: student points to picture of bunny on the desk);
S^R: "That's the bunny!"

Presentation of "difficult" tasks:

S^D: "What does a cat say?" (R: student says, "Meooow.");
S^R: "That's a great cat!" (gives student a whole cookie);
S^D: "What does a cow say?" (R: student says, "Mooooo.");
S^R: "Yeah! A cow says, 'Moooo!'" (tickles student, while handing student a whole cookie); "You may go play!"

End of Session

It helps to think of behavioral momentum as a chain. The instructor is trying to make a long chain and each correct response is a link in the chain. If the instructor does not make it easy to get the chain started, then the chain will never be built. If the instructor gets the chain started but then loses momentum, links are lost or not added to the chain, either because the task is too difficult or the student is not motivated.

One way to ensure that tasks are not too difficult when teaching a new skill, and thus ensure that behavioral momentum is built and maintained, is to engage in task analysis of skills before teaching them. It has been determined through extensive research that children with ASD, in particular, often have great difficulty learning through observation and learning multiple components or multiple steps of an overall skill simultaneously. The reason DTT is used is because it allows skills to be broken down into smaller increments and each increment is taught in isolation. The logic path is as follows: teaching in smaller increments makes achieving mastery more probable, and mastery of skills leads to more success with skill performance, which leads to more and higher levels of reinforcement, which results in higher levels of motivation, which results in an increased momentum of responding correctly to instructions. This comes back to the point that, when deciding which new skill to teach and how, instructors need to make sure they break down skills/tasks into manageable segments, thus making it less difficult for the student to learn and, therefore, enabling instructors to build and maintain behavioral momentum throughout the many teaching sessions they will encounter with a particular student.

Instructors also need to be aware of the ways in which they can also *lose* momentum during a teaching session, whether it be inadvertent or not. This means that the instructor can decrease the momentum by forgetting to implement the different aspects of behavioral momentum, either initially or throughout the teaching session. As discussed previously in the section on reinforcement, instructors must remind themselves that student learning is more a responsibility of the teacher than the student. Thus, when a student becomes noncompliant with responding to instructions or the student begins to provide more incorrect responses than correct responses, the instructor must reevaluate whether she is utilizing all the components of behavioral momentum in order to rebuild momentum to bring the student's correct and compliant responding back on track.

The following are some (but not all) of the ways that instructors can lose behavioral momentum:

- beginning the DTT session with a high level of difficulty task requirement,
- presenting too many difficult tasks in succession,
- giving too few easy tasks at the beginning of the session,
- forgetting to intersperse easy tasks between difficult tasks,
- providing inadequate reinforcement for correct responses to difficult tasks,
- forgetting to provide small amounts of reinforcement for correct responses to easy tasks,
- setting the pace of task presentation too slow (allowing for too much downtime between tasks),
- interrupting the teaching time with reprimands regarding behavior, and
- not maintaining an organized and ordered setting in which tasks are presented.

It is imperative that instructors guard against the loss of behavioral momentum during teaching sessions.

Building and maintaining behavioral momentum with a student during a teaching session provides the instructor with his own teaching momentum. The more the student's behavioral momentum is built and maintained, the easier it will become to teach the student, who will display *fewer* noncompliant behaviors and make *fewer* incorrect responses while acquiring more appropriate skills. This increases the student's motivation to continue engaging in learning activities (both easy and difficult) while also building and maintaining the instructor's overall instructional control and competency in working with the student.

☆ Practice Role-Play Scenario

Have two people work together, one as an instructor and one as a student. Identify a set of easy tasks that the "student" has mastered and a new target (difficult) skill that is to be taught to the student. Have a third person observe and analyze how the instructor performs.

Proceed as follows, with each person practicing

- using the components of behavioral momentum,
- losing momentum through making mistakes (using one of the mistakes listed above), and
- going through the steps of reestablishing instructional control through building behavioral momentum again.

Review the results together. Appendix E provides a behavioral momentum performance evaluation/observation form.

☆ Quick Review: Behavioral Momentum

The cumulative advantages of using the proactive strategy of behavioral momentum are that it allows for and increases the

- pace of the teaching and learning;
- student's fluency of responding (speed plus accuracy);
- success of the student with skill acquisition and compliance with instructions;
- rate of reinforcement, thus maintaining student motivation; and
- instructor's ability to reestablish instructional control if a student stops responding correctly or becomes noncompliant.

Session Management

Session management involves structuring the instruction and work time to maximize opportunities for student learning. Successful session management depends directly on the strength of the instructional control the instructor has established with the student. Instructors who are able to maintain appropriate instructional control are more apt to engage students in positive learning experiences. The following guidelines are offered to help instructors maximize the benefits of each instructional session:

- Establish a specific time for the session and do not vary it greatly.
- Make sure that all reinforcers and learning materials are accessible and ready.
- Minimize distractions as much as possible for both you and the student.
- Pay close attention to the positioning of the student, the materials, and yourself. The student needs to have a clear visual field of the materials (presented in front of him) and needs to be sitting or standing so that he is comfortable and able to reach the materials.
- Take into consideration any sensory issues, age appropriateness, and level of student ability related to the materials that are chosen. For example, a student who consistently places small, roughly textured items in her mouth should not be exposed to such items during training.
- Ensure that you are in an appropriate position to present materials to the student and that you use an appropriate tone of voice and volume for the student to hear and understand you when presenting an S^D.
- Ensure that the instructional and reinforcement times are balanced to maximize learning while maintaining student motivation. Initially, more time and energy should be spent reinforcing the student's efforts and correct responses; gradually, more focus will be placed on obtaining correct responses to S^Ds.
- Focus on making learning positive and fun for the student.
- Engage in playing with reinforcers with the student at appropriate times during the session.
- Mix new and mastered skills throughout the session to maintain the student's success and motivation.
- Reinforce spontaneous, appropriate behavior. Make attempts to catch the little things the student does that are appropriate and are precursors to more important and difficult skills, and surprise him with reinforcement for those behaviors to increase the possibility that they reoccur. For example, if a student is walking down a school hallway and spontaneously points to a picture of a duck on the wall and says, "Duck," you

should get very excited and praise the student and also point to the duck (even if students are supposed to be quiet as they walk down the hallway).

- Always end each session on a positive note by ending either after a time of play with the student or after the reinforcement of a correct response. This will leave a positive memory in the mind of both you and the student and increase the possibility that the next session will be a positive and fun experience.

☆ Practice Role-Play Scenario

Have two people work together as an instructor and a student, or have an instructor work with a real student with ASD. Pick a skill to work on while a third person observes and analyzes how the instructor manages the session. Review the results together. Appendix F provides a session management evaluation/observation form.

☆ Quick Review: Session Management

Successful session management

- enables the instructor to maximize learning;
- depends on the strength of instructional control established;
- engages the student in a positive learning experience;
- occurs in any environment or location, with any materials, and lasts any amount of time; and
- is maximized by employing the preceding guidelines.

Prompting and Fading

Prompting and fading are integral elements of the DTT process. Without prompting and the fading of prompts, a student will neither learn a skill nor be able to independently display the skill. A *prompt* is a stimulus, provided along with an S^D, that aids the student in making a correct response. *Fading* is the systematic withdrawal of prompts. To effectively teach new skills and amend incorrect responses, instructors need to use a variety of prompts and fade them when appropriate. To reiterate, a prompt is used when (a) teaching a new response or skill and (b) correcting a student's incorrect response.

Prompting is one of the most difficult skills for an instructor to master. It often involves a split-second decision about what type of prompt to use or when to use a prompt to ensure a correct response without making a student prompt-dependent. It is recommended that whenever a new prompt is introduced, the instructor immediately begin to plan how it will be faded.

There are many different types of prompts that an instructor can choose to use to assist a student in learning a skill. A list of these prompts follows, with an example of each:

- *Full physical prompt.* The instructor physically manipulates a part of the student's body to assist her with completing a particular action.
  S^D: Instructor says, "Do this." Instructor demonstrates clapping by clapping his hands, then gently puts his hands around the student's wrists and picks up her arms and hands.
  R: Instructor makes the student's hands clap a couple of times.
  S^R: Instructor lets go of the student's wrists and says, "Good clapping, (student's name)."

- *Partial physical prompt.* The instructor physically manipulates a part of the student's body to assist her with starting an action.
  S^D: A pair of scissors and a piece of paper are sitting on the table in front of the student. Instructor says, "Cut the paper" and takes the student's hand and gently places the student's fingers in and around the scissor handles and then lets go.
  R: Student independently completes the action of cutting the paper.
  S^R: Instructor says, "Great cutting, (student's name)."

- *Model/imitative prompt.* The instructor physically demonstrates the action (the correct response) while the student watches.
  S^D: Instructor says, "Clap hands" and claps his own hands as student watches.
  R: Student claps her hands.
  S^R: Instructor says, "Yeah, good clapping."

- *Gestural prompt.* The instructor provides a physical cue to indicate the correct response.
  S^D: There are pictures of different animals on the table in front of the student and instructor. Instructor says, "Give me the dog" and points to the picture of the dog.
  R: Student picks up the picture of the dog and hands it to the instructor.
  S^R: Instructor says, "That's right. This is the dog."

- *Full echoic prompt.* The instructor verbalizes the entire correct response.
  S^D: The instructor holds up a picture of a book in front of the student. Instructor says, "What is it?" and then immediately says, "Book."
  R: Student says, "Book."
  S^R: Instructor says, "Good job. This is a book."

- *Partial echoic prompt.* The instructor verbalizes the *beginning* sound of the correct response.

  S^D: The instructor holds a picture of the student's mom in front of the student. Instructor says, "Who is it?" and then immediately says, "Mmmm."

  R: Student says, "Mommy."

  S^R: Instructor says, "Yes, that is Mommy. Good job, (student's name)."

- *Position prompt.* The instructor places the materials in certain positions (in relationship to the student) to increase the likelihood of the student locating the correct item.

  S^D: The instructor places a red shoe closer to the student than a yellow shoe and a green shoe. Instructor says, "Go get the red shoe."

  R: Student picks up the red shoe and hands it to the instructor.

  S^R: Instructor says, "Good job. You found the red shoe!"

- *Direct verbal prompt.* The instructor provides a verbal instruction to tell the student how to complete one step of a multistep task.

  S^D: Instructor says, "Go wash your hands" and then says, "First, go to the sink."

  R: Student goes to the sink, turns on the water, and washes his hands with soap and water.

  S^R: Instructor says, "Great job washing your hands, (student's name)."

- *Indirect verbal prompt.* The instructor states a question that leads the student to determine the correct response.

  S^D: Instructor says, "Go wash your hands" and then says, "What do you need to do first?"

  R: Student gets up and goes to the sink. He then turns on the water and washes his hands with soap and water.

  S^R: Instructor says, "Nice job washing your hands, (student's name)."

- *Time delay (delay of prompt).* The instructor waits 1–3 seconds after providing the instruction and before providing the prompt to allow the student the opportunity to respond independently.

  S^D: Instructor says, "What color is this?" (while holding up a green toy frog) and then, instead of providing the name of the color immediately (0-second delay) as is done at the beginning of teaching that skill, the instructor waits 1 second with an expectant look on her face while looking at the student.

  R: Student says "Green."

S^R: Instructor says, "Yes! It's green." The next time she will wait 2 seconds and then the next time 3 seconds, and so on, until no prompt is needed.

Note: This type of prompt is an important method that has significant research support relative to preventing prompt-dependency during DTT instruction (MacDuff, Krantz, & McClannahan, 2001).

Deciding on the type of prompt to use will often depend on the type of response being sought. For instance, if a student is being asked to *say* something, the instructor will use a type of *echoic* prompt; if the student is being asked to *do* something, the instructor will use a type of *physical* prompt.

It is also important for an instructor to decide when to use the least intrusive prompt and when to use the most intrusive prompt. The least intrusive prompt is the most subtle prompt from which the student will be able to give the correct response. This is used when (a) the instructor is attempting to fade prompts or (b) the student has already acquired the skill but just made an incorrect response. The most intrusive prompt is the most obvious prompt from which the student will give a correct response. This is used when (a) initially teaching a new skill or (b) engaging in the errorless learning approach. The following are examples of a most intrusive prompt and a least intrusive prompt:

Most Intrusive Prompt

S^D: "Give me the red shoe." Instructor takes the student's hand and puts it on the red shoe.

R: Student picks up the red shoe and hands it to the instructor.

S^R: Instructor says, "Good job. You found the red shoe!"

Least Intrusive Prompt

S^D: "Give me the red shoe." Instructor points to the red shoe.

R: Student picks up the red shoe and hands it to the instructor.

S^R: Instructor says, "Good job. You found the red shoe!"

As stated previously, fading prompts is extremely important. A careful plan needs to be established regarding how a student will be prompted and how the prompts will be faded. Fading prompts ensures that students will not become dependent on the instructor's assistance to complete a task or provide a correct response. The final goal is for students to be able to independently provide a correct response or complete a task within a naturally occurring situation in a typical environment. In the process of fading prompts, the instructor provides higher levels of reinforcement for each correct response that the student provides with less prompting; that is, a less-prompted response receives more reinforcement than a more-prompted response. This will increase the student's motivation to provide better and more independent responses and guard against prompt dependency. Another method of decreasing prompt dependency is to use a variety of prompt styles (decreasing the predictability of certain prompts) with a student. This also makes the learning process more realistic for the student.

It is crucial for instructors to avoid providing inadvertent prompts—thereby unintentionally helping students to make correct responses. Inadvertent prompts can be very subtle and sometimes indistinguishable to the instructor, but not to students. For example, when giving the S^D "Give me the red one," an instructor may inadvertently direct her gaze toward the red item on the table. The student notices that the instructor does this every time she asks for something. As a result, the student learns to wait and watch where the instructor is looking before making a response. It is a good idea for every instructor to be periodically observed by another instructor for inadvertent prompting while working with a student.

It is important to remember that a prompt is part of the discrete trial and should be provided simultaneously with or immediately following the S^D. Furthermore, after a student has given an incorrect response, it is important to restate the original S^D, then provide the prompt, so that the response is given under the control of the S^D and not the prompt.

☆ Practice Role-Play Scenario

Have two people work together as an instructor and a student, or have an instructor work with a real student with ASD. The instructor picks a skill that the student is currently working on but has not yet acquired. A third person observes and analyzes how the instructor prompts the student and fades the prompts throughout the session. Describe the prompts used. Review the results together. Appendix G provides a prompting and fading evaluation/observation form.

☆ Quick Review: Prompting and Fading

Remember to

- establish a careful plan for prompting and fading,
- ensure that the type of prompt used is dependent on the type of response required from the student,
- use the least intrusive prompt possible,
- begin to fade the prompt as soon as possible after introduction,
- make a final goal for the student to be independent of prompts,
- avoid inadvertent prompts,
- provide the prompt simultaneously or immediately following the S^D, and
- restate the original S^D with the prompt if the first response is incorrect.

Shaping

Shaping is developing a new behavior or skill by reinforcing closer and closer approximations of the desired behavior or skill. It is often confused with prompting. Shaping is used when the instructor wants to teach a behavior or skill that a student is not yet able to perform. By systematically requiring closer and closer approximations of the desired behavior (or skill), an instructor is able to systematically move—or shape—a learner's response in the direction of the behavior being sought. An example of when shaping should be used would be when an instructor wants to teach a student to say "cookie." By initially accepting the sound *kee* for "cookie," the instructor can systematically teach the student to make closer and closer approximations of the desired response. Shaping should *not* be used in certain instances: for example, when an instructor wants a student to say "cookie" who has been previously observed to say it, but will not say it when given the S^D "Say *cookie*." Because the latter student is capable of making the sought response, a shaping process involving acceptance of less than the complete utterance would be unacceptable.

There are three steps in the shaping procedure:

1. The instructor identifies the *final* correct response (the *terminal response*)—for example, the ability to say "cookie."
2. The instructor identifies a response to use as a starting point (a behavior the student has the ability to do)—for example, the response "kee."
3. The instructor identifies the steps from the starting point to the final correct response (successive approximations)—for example, (1) "kee," (2) "ooo," (3) "oookee," and (4) "coookeee." These steps may change depending on the student's progress, abilities, and so forth.

It is important to make sure that the steps are small enough that the student can be successful in quickly mastering each new approximation.

The crucial and most difficult part of shaping is requiring the next step in the line of successive instructional approximations. Before an instructor can require the next-closest approximation, he needs to observe the student actually performing that behavior (anywhere and at any time). If the student has never been seen doing what is required, the instructor does not know whether the student can actually do it. When the starting response is occurring reliably and is under the control of the S^D, it is time to introduce and require the next response approximation. When moving to the next response, less reinforcement for the initial response is given, and more reinforcement is provided for attempts and correct responses for the new target approximation. It is important that all instructors working with the student agree and move together to achieve each approximation step. Instructors should also make sure not to remain too long on any one step. Often, failure to achieve a step or to successfully move to the next step occurs because the next step is too difficult, the steps between required actions are too large for the student, the student is not motivated, or the instructor is providing insufficient reinforcement.

☆ Practice Beginning Exercise

Identify a new skill that a student you work with needs to learn or will soon be learning. Write out the terminal response, starting point, successive approximations, and prompts leading to the terminal response.

☆ Practice Role-Play Scenario

Have two people work together as an instructor and a student, or have an instructor work with a real student with ASD. The instructor picks a skill that the student needs to begin learning. A third person observes and analyzes how the instructor shapes the student's responses through reinforcement and increasing the difficulty level of the response. Describe and review together. Appendix H provides a shaping evaluation/observation form.

☆ Quick Review: Shaping

Remember to

- identify the final correct response,
- identify a response to use as a starting point,
- identify the steps from the starting point to the final correct response,
- observe the student performing a behavior correctly before moving to the next approximation or response,
- ensure that all instructors are working on the same tasks, and
- move along as quickly as possible.

When determining a succession of steps for shaping a target behavior, instructors may find it beneficial to consult with appropriate professionals to ensure step suitability. For example, for verbal responses consult with a speech–language pathologist to ensure developmental appropriateness when selecting successive steps.

Chaining

Chaining is another (and oftentimes forgotten) important strategy that behavior analysts use to create the structure needed for students with ASD to learn new skills. Many times the "skill" to be taught to a student is actually a series of behaviors that occur in a sequence. For example, an instructor wants to teach a student to wash her hands; that is, the skill is "washing hands." More specifically, the end result of clean hands requires performing many behaviors in an exact sequence. The following is a sample list of the chain of behaviors that may make up the overall skill of washing hands:

1. Go to the sink.
2. Turn on the water.
3. Put her hands into the water stream so that they get wet.
4. Put soap on her hands.
5. Rub her hands together with the soap.
6. Put her hands under the water to rinse them.
7. Turn off the water.
8. Find or get a towel.
9. Dry her hands on the towel.
10. Put the towel back or throw it away.

In this case there are 10 different behaviors a student needs to learn to perform to accomplish "clean hands." The sequence is equally as important as the list of behaviors. Hands are not dried before they are rubbed with soap and the water is not turned off before the hands are rinsed. Also, none of the 10 steps/behaviors can be omitted to successfully "wash hands" even though, technically, the hands may be clean without turning off the water or drying them; however, there will be unfortunate results for leaving the water running or going back to doing something with wet hands. Therefore, when teaching a student to wash her hands, the instructor needs to teach and reinforce the correct and independent performance of each of the 10 different behaviors that result in the overall skill of "washing hands."

This example also demonstrates that chaining is different from shaping. As discussed previously (in the section on shaping), when using the shaping strategy to teach a skill, the instructor reinforces the successive approximations that a student demonstrates to eventually successfully perform *one* behavior (e.g., saying "cookie"). In chaining, the successive behaviors are reinforced in a sequential chain toward an end result of acquiring a complex skill. This is called a *behavior chain*. Behavior chains are very important to everyone, but people can grow up without learning how to perform some crucial behavior chains and, therefore, are not capable of gaining important skills, such as riding a bike or swimming.

Another important aspect of chaining is that each behavior in a specific behavior chain sequence serves as a cue for the next behavior; that is, performing one behavior signals what behavior should be performed next. This is helpful when teaching a person a new skill. Oftentimes certain sequences can be learned very quickly because the steps in the chain are logical and make sense; for example, when a person has wet hands, she typically has the urge to dry them (even if it is just to wipe them on her shirt or pants), and thus it is easier to teach her the behavior of "drying hands." In other situations, the steps in a behavior chain may not necessarily be a prompt to perform the next step. For example, sitting on a bike does not logically prompt a child to then lift up his feet and put them on the pedals. The child needs to be taught to lift his feet and shown how to do it.

When behavior chaining is employed to teach a child to ride a bike or to swim, there are often steps that are difficult to learn and can even cause fear. For example, lifting one's feet up off the ground to balance on the bike or putting one's head under water to swim could evoke fear. Instructors need to take this into consideration and provide a much higher level of reinforcement for performing these types of difficult or fear-inducing steps. Sometimes, one step/behavior in a long chain can take a while to learn. In such cases, shaping (reinforcement of successive approximations) is used to teach that one behavior. Differential reinforcement, as previously discussed (in the reinforcement section), may be used to assist learners acquire the more difficult steps/behaviors in a behavior chain.

There are two types of behavior chaining: forward chaining and backward chaining. Forward chaining is self-explanatory. When teaching a new skill, the instructor starts with teaching the first behavior in the behavior chain, then teaches each subsequent behavior in sequence (hence, moving "forward"). Sometimes this means focusing on teaching and reinforcing the first behavior in the chain and then, when the student learns the first behavior, teaching the next behavior, and so on, while always prompting the student through the rest of the steps in that behavior chain to complete the chain process. For example, this would mean that the instructor completes all the steps when working on "washing hands." The student does not stop and leave the sink once he has learned to turn on the water; instead, the instructor always follows through with the rest of the steps by helping the student finish the chain every time, and thus the learner has clean hands at the end of the chain of "washing hands." Other times, it means the instructor focuses on and teaches the first behavior in the chain and does not proceed with any more of the behaviors in that chain until the student has successfully learned that first behavior. For example, with swimming, getting in and being in the water might be the only behavior that an instructor would initially work on.

Backward chaining means that the instructor focuses on and teaches the student to independently perform the last step in the chain first; when the last step is mastered, the student is taught the second-to-last step, and so on, until the entire chain is learned. This strategy is often used to help the student understand the overall end result of the chain. Moreover, by performing and learning the last step, the student is more motivated to then learn the entire chain of behaviors because the end result is so desirable. For example, teaching a child to complete puzzles is typically achieved more quickly and with more fun (motivation) by using backward chaining. The puzzle pieces are all in the puzzle except for the last piece and the child is taught to put in the last piece and thus see the entire completed puzzle. Once the child performs that behavior independently, the child is taught to put in the last two pieces, and so on.

Backward chaining can also be more effective than forward chaining when it comes to teaching very complex behavior chains, such as teaching a child to tie shoes or get dressed. The instructor performs all the beginning steps/behaviors and then the child learns to perform the last step; for example, tying the final loop in the shoelaces or pulling on the shirt. These behavior chains permit the child to be part of the behavior chain as it occurs, by watching and/or feeling the steps and hearing the instructor label all the steps leading up to the last one. Then, by having the learner perform the last step, the last two steps, and so forth, the instructor ensures that the child has successfully completed the task (i.e., finished the entire behavior chain) and has seen all the other steps performed correctly. Many times backward chaining is used as a part of errorless learning because the nature of a particular overall skill is so complex. Thus, teaching the behaviors in backward order makes the student's rate and probability of success much higher. Also, the highest level of reinforcement that the child receives ends up always being after the entire behavior chain has been completed. In this manner, the student is further motivated to successfully complete the entire chain.

Choosing whether to use forward chaining or backward chaining is based solely on the needs of the student who is being taught the skill. Often the decision is obvious. For example, swimming cannot be taught by using backward chaining. Other times, an instructor may decide to use forward chaining because engaging the child and getting her involved in a particular behavior chain might be important to the child and, therefore, the instructor wants to reinforce her for doing the first step. This will motivate her to attend to and learn the next step, and so forth. At other times, a student may need to see the overall picture to be motivated to learn (i.e., in cases involving a whole-to-part learner rather than a part-to-whole learner). In these instances, any behavior chain that can be taught through backward chaining should be done in that manner with that student.

The example of hand washing is a behavior that can essentially be taught through either forward chaining or backward chaining. The instructor can teach and highly reinforce the student for performing the first step and then use physical prompting to help the student complete the rest of the steps/behaviors in the chain in sequence. After learning the first step/behavior, the student then moves on to the second step, and so forth. Or the instructor may start with physically prompting the student through all the steps of the chain, then teach and reinforce the last step, and move backward until, lastly, the first step is taught. When chaining-choice decisions are flexible, they should be based on what is best for the student relative to his learning abilities and how best to optimize motivation for learning more difficult tasks.

Essential guidelines instructors should follow when planning to teach a behavior chain to a student follow:

1. Clearly define the target skill and each of the behaviors in the chain.
2. Use differential reinforcement while progressing through the chain of behaviors.
3. Monitor the student's progress.

The target skill (e.g., washing hands) needs to be clearly defined, as well as the individual steps/behaviors in the chain that will comprise the overall target skill. If these are not clearly defined, the various instructors or the student can easily become lost, confused, or sidetracked while working on the behavior chain. One instructor might teach a behavior that other instructors are not teaching and/or reinforcing or might teach one of the steps in one way while other instructors reinforce in a different way. Saying "We are working on washing hands" may seem self-explanatory, and it might be assumed the steps/behaviors in the chain are understood by everyone. This is not the case when working with students with disabilities, and in particular those with ASD. Each step/behavior needs to be carefully analyzed and stated to ensure there are not two to three behaviors within a particular step/behavior and, therefore, that more steps are needed for the child to be successful as he completes the easier and smaller tasks. Only by ensuring that this process is carefully in place will instructors be in a position to create the momentum needed to teach a behavior chain.

Consider the list of 10 behaviors that were provided for teaching "washing hands" at the beginning of this section. There may be steps that were left out or need to be broken down into smaller steps for one child; for another child, some steps may best be combined to facilitate learning. For example, for one child, the step of "put soap on hands" may need to be broken down into smaller steps/behaviors, for instance, if a pump soap dispenser is used. The step "get the step stool and put in front of sink" may need to be added as the first step if the child is small and cannot reach the faucet. If this circumstance is not analyzed, one instructor may always be getting the stool for the student and then saying "Wash your hands," thus having great success with the student performing the successive steps in the chain, whereas another instructor is saying "Wash your hands," but first prompting the child to get the stool on which to stand. In this situation, the two instructors have not progressed beyond the step that allows them to work on the rest of the chain. If another instructor then says, "Wash your hands," but stands there and waits for the child to start washing his hands without knowing that the other two instructors have included getting the stool, the student may do nothing and the instructor will be confused. The instructor may then proceed through the error correction procedure, thinking the student is not responding. As discussed throughout this book, when working with children with ASD, task analysis is absolutely essential with every skill and behavior and is central to successful use of DTT.

Differential reinforcement is also crucial to successfully teaching a behavior chain to a student. When one specific step/behavior in a chain is being taught, *that* particular step is the one for which the student receives the highest level of reinforcement. When the student has learned to independently perform that step without error, the student no longer receives a high amount of reinforcement for performing that behavior (except for praise). The next step in the chain now becomes the target behavior and the one for which the student receives the most reinforcement. Also, if one step/behavior in the chain is always more difficult to do than other behaviors, the student will always receive more reinforcement for performing *that* behavior. The key is to always keep the student attending and motivated to want to perform the next or the more difficult behavior because she will get that higher and better reinforcement for doing that next step.

It is also important to remember that students need to be reinforced for performing each *individual* step and *all* the steps in the correct *order*. If the instructor tells the child to "Wash your hands" and the child gets his hands wet and then dries them, he has completed *some of the steps* and in the correct order. Yet he did not complete the entire behavior chain of washing hands. Thus *no* reinforcement is provided and the student needs to start over and complete all the steps in that behavior chain. Also, it is crucial to reinforce only the particular step/behavior when it is performed in the correct order *within* the entire chain. For example, if an instructor is teaching the step/behavior "rub hands together with the soap," he does not teach and reinforce this behavior in isolation outside of the chain of "washing hands," *nor* does the instructor reinforce this behavior if the student walks into the bathroom and simply rubs his hands together with soap.

Finally, it is important to collect data on all the steps/behaviors in the behavior chain to continually monitor the progress, or lack of, that the student makes. This is not only to see if he is acquiring the steps, but also to make sure all the correct steps/behaviors in the chain have been successfully identified and broken down into easily mastered steps. If the student is not doing well at a particular stage in the chain, it typically means that the instructors have erred in the task analysis or how the step/behavior is being taught. It is always imperative that the instructors first analyze what they may have possibly done incorrectly before assuming the student is unable to learn or should bear full responsibility for not performing correctly. Data can also assist in identifying if certain instructors are achieving more success than others. This can sometimes mean that the definition of the target skill or behaviors in the chain has not been defined clearly enough and those instructors who are "showing" more success are accepting and reinforcing different or less difficult behaviors than other instructors. Sometimes some instructors are truly more successful at working on behavior chains with students and should take a lead role in that process. It is also sometimes the case that students cannot initially generalize working on a behavior chain with all their instructors and need to work on a task with one person, then two, and so on.

Another helpful strategy to use when teaching behavior chains to students with ASD is to use pictures to show all the steps in the process. The pictures are cut out, laminated, and placed on a Velcro strip used as a visual schedule so the student can see the steps. This makes the set of steps concrete and permanent and allows the student to see each behavior in isolation. It often works best if the pictures show the student herself performing each behavior. As the student performs each step, either independently or by prompting, the student removes the picture of the behavior just completed and places it in a "finished" box. This helps the student know what to do next without the instructor having to continually either verbally or physically prompt the next step (of course, this is not to say that the instructor may not still have to use additional verbal, physical, or gestural prompts along with the picture schedule). Eventually, the visuals can be faded so that the student performs the whole behavior chain without needing any prompts.

Chaining is a very useful tool in the overall DTT process when working with students with ASD, particularly for teaching self-help and functional-living skills. These self-help skills and performing everyday common tasks and routines can be very difficult and complex for individuals with ASD. Using chaining can make teaching these important tasks manageable for the instructors and attainable for the individual learning them. It is imperative to remember that some students may never learn to perform an entire behavior chain successfully or independently, but with the assistance of visuals or another person providing minimal support/prompting, they can become as independent as possible. For example, an individual "doing laundry" may be able to collect the clothes and bring them into the laundry room, yet always need help sorting them into correct piles for washing. With assistance and prompting on some difficult-to-learn steps, the learner may proceed and independently put the clothes into the washing machine, measure out and pour in the correct amount of detergent, close the lid, choose the correct setting on the buttons, and start the load. This is a huge success and a significant step in the direction of independence and possible self-worth for that individual. The learner in this scenario might always need help in sorting clothes for washing; however, in no way does this need diminish the achievement of successfully performing the behavior chain.

☆ Practice Beginning Exercise

Each person identifies a self-help or adaptive behavior skill that is important for all people to learn. Break it down into the sequence of smaller/individual skills that a person has to learn to complete the overall skill. Write out the sequence and then practice going through the motions so that you are sure that you have not forgotten a step/skill in the sequence from start to finish. Provide reasoning for why you might use backward chaining for a given student and forward chaining for another student.

☆ Practice Role-Play Scenario

Two people practice together as an instructor and a student with ASD. Go through the process of using forward chaining or backward chaining to teach one of the skills identified in the practice exercise. Determine ahead of time what you will reinforce, what your prompts will be, and so forth. Use the checklist provided in Appendix A (task analysis) and the checklist in the Quick Review section for task analysis plus chaining to ensure that you follow all the necessary requirements of chaining.

☆ Quick Review

Chaining is used to teach an overall skill that includes several smaller skills/behaviors that must be completed in a sequence and consists of two different types: forward chaining and backward chaining.

Teach the behavior chain/steps to the student using the following process:

- clearly define the target skill and each of the behaviors in the chain,
- use visual supports when teaching each step and showing the entire chain,
- use differential reinforcement while progressing through the chain of behaviors,
- monitor the student's progress through data collection, and
- adjust each step as needed to ensure success with learning.

Error Correction Procedure

The error correction procedure is a consequence for an incorrect response or failure to respond following the presentation of an S^D. The error correction procedure is a component of errorless learning; it strengthens the connection between the S^D and the response by increasing the likelihood that the response will be correct. It involves using prompts and fading prompts to obtain the correct response. Instead of saying "no" when a student provides an incorrect response and moving on to another trial, the instructor uses the opportunity to engage the errorless learning approach and teach the correct response. The goal of the error correction procedure is to obtain the correct response under the control of an unprompted S^D. It is important to remember that this procedure is used only with skills that the student has acquired; it is not used when teaching a new skill.

This procedure is the most difficult to learn when using the DTT process and the most difficult to use when teaching a student a specific skill. As such, instructors need to practice this skill many times and continue to practice it until it becomes an automatic component of the DTT process.

Implementation of the error correction procedure begins once an incorrect response has been provided by the student and involves the following five steps:

Step 1. The instructor restates the original SD.

- If the student now provides a *correct* response, the student is reinforced appropriately and the procedure ends.
- If the response is *incorrect*, the instructor and student continue to Step 2.
- If there is *no response*, the instructor must make sure she has the student's attention and then state the original S^D a second time. If the student provides a correct response, it is reinforced appropriately and the procedure ends. If there is still no response or an incorrect response, the instructor and student continue to Step 2.

Step 2. The instructor adjusts the prompt level until the student successfully provides a correct response. The instructor repeats the S^D and provides the least intrusive prompt.

- If the student provides a *correct* response, the instructor reinforces the student appropriately (but not with the highest level of reinforcement) and then proceeds backward (fading the prompts) by steps to the last unprompted S^D.
- If the student provides an *incorrect* response with this prompt, the S^D is repeated and a prompt is provided that is slightly stronger than the previous prompt.
- If there is *no response*, the instructor follows the same procedure as if the response was incorrect.

Step 3. The instructor presents the original unprompted SD. Depending on the student and the level and number of prompts provided to acquire the correct response in Step 2, the instructor will typically use a discrete trial to fade each prompt before providing the original S^D without any prompts.

- When the instructor finally provides the original S^D without any prompts and the student provides a *correct* response, the instructor needs to provide a high level of reinforcement, including praise.
- If the instructor provides the unprompted S^D and the student provides *no response* or an *incorrect* response, the instructor must return to Step 2 and work back to the previous unprompted S^D in order to obtain a correct response.

Step 4. The instructor provides a "distractor" trial. This is a trial that involves requesting the student to perform an easy and already acquired skill before once again returning to the target skill. The instructor provides the S^D for the distractor trial, obtains the correct response, and then provides a low level of reinforcement (matching the easy level of the response being required).

Step 5. The instructor once again provides the original unprompted SD for the target skill. If the instructor obtains a correct response, a high level of reinforcement is provided to the student. This trial ensures that the student can still provide the correct response to the unprompted S^D subsequent to a period of time and a distraction following the last S^D presentation. Later in the work session, it is beneficial to again provide this S^D to make sure the student is still able to provide a correct response.

It is recommended that instructors also use the following techniques during the error correction procedure:

- Before presenting an S^D, make sure that the student is attending and motivated and that the appropriate reinforcers are readily available.
- Restate the S^D before each new prompt is provided, so that the correct response is connected to and under the control of the S^D and not the prompt (to prevent the student from becoming prompt-dependent).
- Reinforce every correct response. Regardless of the level of prompt provided, reinforcement must be provided for each correct response so that the student's efforts are acknowledged and she remains motivated to continue responding.
- Provide less reinforcement for any prompted responses.
- Save the most powerful reinforcer for the correct, unprompted responses, especially the correct response after the distractor trial.

If responses are not proceeding well with the error correction procedure, the instructor may need to end the session on the most independent response and evaluate the session. When attempting to determine the difficulty, instructors are encouraged to consider varying the

- level of prompting,
- type of prompts,
- type and strength of the reinforcer, and/or
- task being required of the student (e.g., its level of difficulty).

Recent research (McGahn & Lerman, 2013) has suggested that not all students with ASD respond the same way to the same error correction procedure or benefit from its use. While all DTT programs need to use error correction procedures, it is possible that different students may benefit from different procedures. Some researchers (Coon & Miguel, 2012; Worsdell et al., 2005) are also investigating different factors that they are finding influence a student's response and benefit from a certain type of error correction procedure, for example, prior learning history and the function of the procedure (e.g., do the prompts serve as an aversive stimuli?). While this research is still recent and sometimes conflicting, and conclusions are still being drawn, it is important for DTT program supervisors to understand that it may be beneficial to do an initial assessment with each student with ASD to identify the most appropriate error correction procedure for that student. The different procedures used with children with ASD include (a) active student response (ASR) instruction, (b) no response (NR) instruction, (c) direct rehearsal (DR), (d) vocal feedback, and (e) modeling. The goal in choosing a procedure for a given student is to select the one that produces skill mastery in the fewest number of trials. The error correction procedure discussed in this section is the direct rehearsal procedure, which continues to be supported by research as a procedure that is effective with most students with ASD (McGahn & Lerman, 2013).

☆ Practice Role-Play Scenario

Have two people work together as an instructor and a student, or have an instructor work with a real student with ASD. Pick a skill that the student has almost acquired. Practice using the error correction procedure for incorrect responses made by the student. A third person observes and analyzes how the instructor implements the error correction procedure. Describe and discuss together. Appendix I provides an error correction procedure evaluation/observation form.

☆ Quick Review: Error Correction Procedure

Remember to

- use only with skills that the student has already acquired;
- use the five-step process:
  1. restate the original S^D and go to Step 2 only if no response or an incorrect response is made
  2. adjust the prompt level until the student provides the correct response
  3. present the original unprompted S^D and obtain a correct response
  4. provide a "distractor" trial
  5. provide the original unprompted S^D again and obtain a correct response
- ensure that the student is attending and motivated;
- restate the S^D before each new prompt;
- reinforce every correct response; and
- save the most powerful reinforcer for correct, unprompted responses.

Figure 1 provides a diagram of the error correction procedure, including the steps and the decision-making process that instructors are advised to follow.

Transfer Trial

As previously discussed, it is important that the goal for teaching students with ASD, including through the use of DTT, be to provide them with the skills they need to become more independent in their daily living. Many times instructors do not focus enough on fading their prompts or fading their prompts quickly enough, causing a child to become prompt-dependent. One method for fading prompts or for providing prompts that are less intrusive is to use what is called the *transfer trial*.

The processes of prompting and fading and the error correction procedure were discussed in detail in previous sections. It may be helpful to note at this point that transfer trials are essentially the trials that an instructor uses to progress the child toward independent responses; that is, the instructor uses the trials to transfer the student from prompted responding to independent responding. Within the error correction procedure, those trials occur in Step 2, wherein the instructor is adjusting and fading prompts, and thus transferring trials.

When teaching a new skill, the instructor may start with one or two discrete trials that essentially prompt the student with the correct response and offer a bridge to the next S^D. Below is an example in which the instructor is planning to teach a student to expressively label the colors of objects. The student has already mastered the skill of receptively identifying the colors of objects.

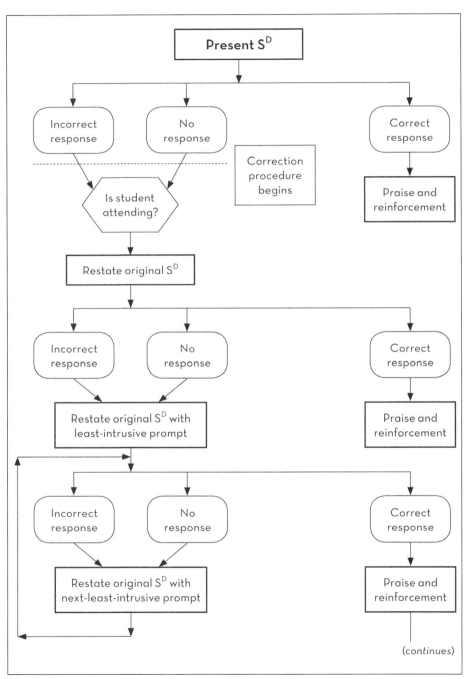

Figure 1. Diagram of the error correction procedure, including the decision-making process.

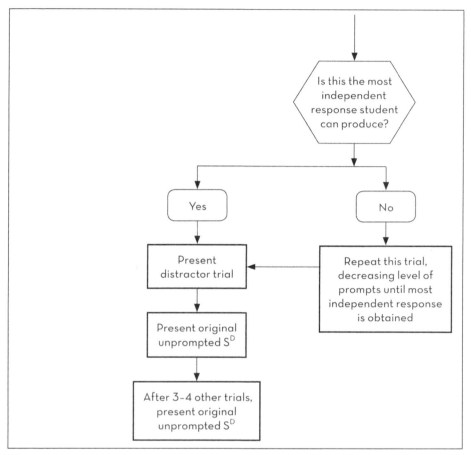

Figure 1. (*continued*)

Transfer Trial (receptive ID of colors of objects)

S^D: There are five colored objects in front of the student, and the instructor says, "Give me the red one."

R: The student reaches out, picks up a red car, and puts it in the instructor's hand.

S^R: Instructor says, "That's right! That's the red one!"

Inter-Trial Interval

New Skill Trial (expressive ID of colors of objects)

S^D: Instructor holds up the same red car and says, "What color is it?"

R: Student says, "Red."

S^R: Instructor says, "Yes! It is red. Give me five!"

The transfer trial was a discrete trial that used an already acquired skill to essentially "prompt" the student to attend to the color of an object, specifically, the color red. Because the student heard the instructor ask for the red one, and the student successfully receptively identified the red one and gave it to the instructor, the student is now more likely to know to say "red" when the instructor holds up the red car and asks the student what color it is. It is one of the maximally least intrusive types of prompts that an instructor can use—an already mastered skill used to teach a new skill.

Another benefit for using such a trial is that, within a teaching session, instructors are always working to maintain behavioral momentum (interspersing easy/mastered tasks with more difficult tasks). In this connection, transfer trials help to build or maintain behavioral momentum because an easy/mastered task, one with which the student is successful, is used to promote success with a more difficult trial.

☆ Practice Role-Play Scenario

Have two people work together as an instructor and a student. Pick a skill that the student has already acquired and a skill that will be taught as a new skill. The mastered skill needs to be one that naturally precedes learning the new skill. Together, work on how you would use the mastered skill to create a transfer trial in teaching the new skill.

☆ Quick Review: Transfer Trial

Transfer trials are used as

- one of the least intrusive methods for providing a prompt to a student, and
- a means to provide less of a prompt than what was provided before and to bridge the gap between a larger prompt and no prompt.

Token Economy Systems

Detailed information about and descriptions of the types and uses of reinforcement have been provided earlier in the book. Being able to work and wait for reinforcement (delayed reinforcement) is another important skill for all students with ASD to learn, including as they get older and learn functional living skills. This is especially true if parents and professionals wish for a student to be successful in a less restrictive setting (i.e., a general education classroom) for some or part of the student's education. Individual token economy systems may still be used in a general education classroom, but the consistent use of immediate 1:1

reinforcement with primary reinforcers is not tolerated or accepted in a general education classroom.

The aim of a token economy system is to teach the student how to delay reinforcement while maintaining appropriate learning behavior. As previously mentioned, primary reinforcers are often used when DTT teaching begins because they are concrete, tangible, and what young children desire the most (e.g., food, drink). Eventually it is important for students, as for all people, to be able to work for longer periods of time to gain reinforcement, and for them to learn how to do so, instructors need to systematically plan for delayed and intermittent patterns of reinforcement.

To make the transition from primary to secondary reinforcers, instructors need to pair secondary reinforcers with the primary reinforcers so that the student learns that the secondary reinforcer is also desirable and something he likes and wants. In the case of a token economy, instructors begin by giving the child a token and then teaching the student to immediately exchange it for something the student wants, for example, a piece of cookie or a drink of juice. At first, the token means nothing, but the child learns that he can earn these tokens and then use them to get what he really wants. Instructors also do this by pairing tokens with things like praise, tickles, and high-fives (all secondary reinforcers), so that the token gains power in and of itself as a great thing to earn. This is in addition to the power the token has to "buy" something that the student really wants (such as a primary reinforcer) when the student is motivated for other forms of reinforcement. Eventually, some students want to earn tokens to earn a secondary reinforcer, which is the instructor's goal. Playing with someone, reading a book, playing with a toy, and so forth are all things that are much more socially significant, meaningful, and functional.

Therefore, when implementing a token economy system, instructors initially allow for the continuation of 1:1 reinforcement in the form of tokens and praise, while requiring the student to maintain appropriate behavior with less frequent access to preferred items. Gradually, the student is required to produce a greater amount of work for a longer period of time before gaining access to preferred items or activities. The goal is for the student to complete a specific number of work tasks or work for a certain amount of time and provide correct responding with appropriate behaviors.

The important factor in a token economy system is what is reinforced. It needs to be clear to the student what he is earning a token for. When the instructor hands the token to the student, she needs to tell the student why he is receiving the token; that should be the target behavior that the instructor is trying to increase. Recent research (Fiske et al., 2015; Hackenberg, 2009) discusses the benefits and effectiveness of having a set of "rules" for appropriate learning behavior targets the student needs to display and that result in earning a token. In other words, the student does not earn a token only for responding correctly, but for responding correctly *and* behaving appropriately. This assists with teaching appropriate learning behaviors alongside teaching new skills, while also ensuring that the student is not reinforced for a correct response while also flicking his fingers in front of his face. This means that if a student provides the correct response of "Red" for the instructor's question of "What color is it?", he does not earn the token unless he also has his hands down.

No more than two to three target-appropriate learning behaviors (rules) should be targeted at once, so that it is not too difficult for the student to earn tokens. It is important that the "rules" (target-appropriate learning behaviors) be individualized for each student's own needs. It is also important to prioritize the target behaviors that are most impeding the student's learning. The following are two examples:

1. A student with moderate to severe autism regularly bangs on the table with his hands, makes humming noises, stomps his feet, and picks at things. In this scenario, the instructor could target banging on the table first. Thus, the rule would be "You need hands down." Humming would later be added to the rules: "You need to have hands down and a quiet mouth." Later, if the student no longer engages in banging on the table, the rules might change to "You need a quiet mouth and feet down."
2. A student with mild to moderate autism regularly tries to run away from the desk (elope), throws things on the floor, and ignores teacher instructions. In this case, the instructor could target all three behaviors at once. The rules would be "You need to sit, follow instructions, and have hands down."

Following is the procedure for implementing a token economy system with a student. An example of what a token board looks like is included in Appendix J.

1. At the beginning of each teaching session, the instructor sets up the student's token economy board. The board includes
   a. a picture for each of the rules at the top of the board,
   b. a space to attach the chosen reinforcer that the student is working for, and
   c. spaces for individual tokens to be attached.
2. The student must follow these rules (appropriate learning behaviors) while working at his desk:
   a. Rule #1 (e.g., quiet mouth)
   b. Rule #2 (e.g., hands down)
3. A reinforcement sampling (as previously discussed) must take place based on two criteria:

    a. at the start of each session, and

    b. approximately every hour or any time behavioral momentum has been lost.

4. Prior to starting each DTT learning drill or set of drills (depending on the targeted level), the instructor reviews the desired behaviors (rules) required for the learner to earn reinforcement. This should resemble something like "First do your work, with a quiet mouth, and then play with (item)." This phrase should be said while the instructor points first to the pictures of the rules at the top of the board and then to the reinforcer(s) the student is working to receive shown at the bottom of the board.

5. Once the token economy board has been set up and reviewed, the instructor may begin the drill work.

    a. The instructor should always start with easy tasks to build behavioral momentum.

    b. For each correct response the student provides while following the rules, the instructor gives the student a token and states the rule(s) that was followed, for example, "(Student's name), you did great work with a quiet mouth." The instructor does not have to state every rule every time, but should state at least one rule each time.

        i. During the beginning phases of the program, reinforcement should be provided on a 1:1 basis for all target skills and typically on a 4:1 basis for mastered skills.

        ii. As the student becomes more fluent with the token economy system, the reinforcement schedule is systematically faded to eventually become intermittent.

6. Initially, the student is required to work for one token. This phase teaches the correspondence between receiving a token and gaining access to a preferred item or other forms of reinforcement. As the student meets with success with the token economy system, the number of tokens required to earn a reinforcer is gradually increased.

7. It is important that the student clearly understand when she has earned the target number of tokens needed for reinforcement and is finished with the work session. The goal is that the student would eventually see the five or 10 tokens needed to earn reinforcement and initiate taking the tokens off the token board, handing them to the instructor, and pointing to the reinforcer or saying "time to (reinforcer)." Thus, once the student has earned all of the required tokens, the instructor should wait a few seconds to see if the student either:

    a. takes the tokens off the board and hands them to the instructor
    OR

   b. asks for or points to the reinforcement item (the student is then
      prompted to first give the instructor the tokens)
      Note: Doing one of these two things signifies that the student under-
      stands that by engaging in these behaviors he gets the item in ex-
      change for the tokens. If he does not reach for the tokens or point to
      the picture of the reinforcer, he should be prompted to do so.
8. Initially, work sessions should be short in duration to permit exchanging only one, two, or three tokens. This may mean that a particular block of trials needs to be broken into smaller chunks. Al-
   though this is *not* ideal at the beginning, it *must* happen in order to
   teach the token economy concept. This also means that small
   amounts of the reinforcer that the student is earning are used, because the learner is exchanging only one or two tokens for it. As she
   exchanges more tokens, she can earn more time with the reinforcer or
   more of the reinforcer.
9. If at any point the student is not following a rule, the instructor will
   a. state "That's not (rule),"
   b. continue with easy and less demanding tasks until the student is
      calm and ceases engagement in inappropriate behaviors,
   c. review the token economy rules by stating "To get the (item), you
      need to (rule)," and
   d. continue with instruction.
10. Data needs to be taken, at least two to three times per day, on whether
    the student earns the tokens by engaging in appropriate behaviors
    (target rules). These data will be used to determine when and how the
    student will progress through the steps of the token economy.

First-Then Visual Supports

First-then visual supports are used to provide clear expectations to the student
about what is happening and what will happen next. Sometimes a first-then visual support is used as a simple schedule that the student is shown to follow in
the moment, for example, "First you need to hang up your coat (picture of coat
on a hook) and then go to the bathroom (picture of a toilet)." Other times, and
more commonly, a visual support is used to show the student, who really wants
a cracker right now, that first he needs to hang up his coat (picture of coat on a
hook) and then he can have a cracker (picture of a cracker).
   Students with ASD who are early learners often need this type of visual support before they can begin to use and understand a token economy system. The
prerequisite skill/concept of "I need to do something *you* want me to do before I

can do something *I* want to do" needs to be acquired prior to a learner being able to use a typical token system. Some early learners may get very upset when a reinforcer is taken away because they think it is completely gone. They often have not yet developmentally acquired *object permanence*; when they cannot see something, they do not understand that it is still there. By using the system of teaching first this and then that, while pointing to the visuals, instructors help students understand that they need to wait for the reinforcer, do something first, and then they can have the desired item/activity. The visual support picture in Figure 2 shows that an item/reinforcer is not gone and that it will come back contingent upon an appropriate behavior; it is often very helpful with young and early-stage learners.

The first-then system is used throughout all instructional portions of a student's day.

1. The board should show
   a. a picture of a task, for example, sitting at a desk,
   b. pictures of a student's rule(s) under the task, and
   c. pictures of reinforcers that the student chooses.
2. A reinforcement sampling must take place
   a. at the start of each session,
   b. every 30 minutes,
      AND/OR
   c. if the student shows signs of disinterest in the chosen reinforcer.
3. For open-ended activities, a timer is used to create a leveling progression system (e.g., first 1 minute, then 2 minutes).
4. For close-ended activities, the transition to "then" (i.e., the reinforcement is earned and the task has been completed) can occur at the

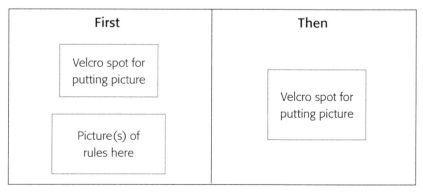

Figure 2. A visual support picture.

natural end of a task or after the end of a certain amount of close-ended tasks.

5. Prior to each task/set of drills, the instructor should review the appropriate behaviors (rules) required to earn the reinforcer. This should resemble something like "First sitting at the desk, then (reinforcer)."

6. When the amount of time that the student is required to sit and do tasks exceeds 1 minute, other supplemental reinforcement should be used (e.g., a small piece of food) for correct responding with (rule) to maintain the student's motivation to wait for the larger reinforcer.

7. Once the timer goes off, or the close-ended task has been completed, signaling the end of the work, the student should exchange the picture of the reinforcer for the actual reinforcer. This can be facilitated by the student's
   a. removing the picture of the item and handing it to the instructor— a verbal prompt may be needed to facilitate the exchange; or
   b. verbally requesting the item—in this instance a physical prompt may be needed to initiate the physical exchange of the picture with the request.

8. Data should be taken two to three times a day regarding the student's success in using the system. Once the student demonstrates that he is no longer distressed by the give and take of reinforcers relative to doing work tasks and can sit for about 5 minutes consistently to work for a reinforcer, the transition to using a formal token economy system can begin.

It should be noted that the first-then visual support system may also be a way to fade out the need for any visual token economy system. Many students will begin to demonstrate that they understand the overall concept of first doing a work task and then getting a reinforcer after they are done. They do not show the desire or need to earn tokens to maintain their motivation and follow their progress toward finishing work and earning the reinforcer. It is possible that a student can be shown a general visual of first-then (with rules), sit and work for 20 minutes or so (while still receiving intermittent praise for appropriate behavior and work), and then be told "Great sitting and doing your work; you can now have (reinforcer)."

Ideally a supervisor (a BCBA or a BCaBA, a Board Certified Associate Behavioral Analyst) will be available to guide each student's DTT program. Such a supervisor will have training in implementing token economy systems and will guide the overall teaching process and create individualized procedures for the steps used to teach the token economy system and/or first-then visual support with a student with ASD. Token economy systems and rules need to be continually adjusted in accordance with the tasks and concepts that the student learns quickly and those that the student struggles to learn.

☆ Practice Beginning Exercise

Each person works alone to identify a couple of difficulties that a student can often demonstrate and which can often affect the student's ability to successfully participate in learning activities.

1. Draw or make a token board that displays the rules for that child to earn tokens.
2. Make a spot for a picture or word to be put to indicate what reinforcer the student is earning.
3. Make tokens that you can use during a teaching session.

☆ Practice Role-Play Scenario

Have two people work together as an instructor and a student. Utilizing the above procedure for teaching a student using a token system, set up a teaching session with mastered and target skills and work through all the steps and phases of the token economy procedure to gain practice with the entire process. If available, a third person can observe the session and provide feedback regarding the instructor's implementation of the system. Appendix K provides a token economy system evaluation/observation form.

☆ Quick Review

When using token economy systems, instructors need to

- use only two to three rules at a time as target appropriate learning behaviors,
- use reinforcement sampling frequently enough to know the highest level reinforcer the student wants,
- review the rules with the student before each teaching session,
- use behavioral momentum to start the student earning tokens easily and to maintain student engagement during the session,
- praise the student using specific language about the rules he is following,
- tell the student when he is not following the rules,
- have the student physically exchange the tokens for the reinforcer,
- gradually increase the difficulty for earning tokens as the student progresses with learning,
- take data on the student's progress, and
- use a first-then system if needed when first teaching a student to delay reinforcement or when fading out the use of a token economy system.

Discrimination Training

Learning to identify and label items in the environment is a skill that is gained and improved upon with development and maturity. Typically, it is learned through observing others and asking questions. Many children with ASD do not go through this developmental process and do not naturally learn to discriminate items from one another and the labels/names that go with them. DTT is used to facilitate discrimination training, the procedure that teaches children to distinguish one item (or response) from another.

Discrimination is a foundational skill that all people need in order to communicate with others, follow directions, label items and actions and emotions, read, follow a schedule, and learn self-care skills, to name just a few areas. Students with ASD have difficulty learning to discriminate, and it is difficult to control which elements of each item/stimulus students need to attend to. Therefore, to effect the correct responses students need to make when a particular S^D is given, instructors need to be careful how the skill is taught and what stimuli/materials (of which there are many) are used.

In this regard it is important that instructors always evaluate the *control* that the *stimulus* has over the student's *behavior.* For example, the instructor might say, "What color is that?" (while pointing to a red ball that has a green block sitting next to it) and the student says, "Red." In this case the instructor can reasonably conclude that the student is *discriminating* or *responding differentially.* This means that the learner could have said (but did not say) "ball" or "green" or "block," and so on. This demonstrates the control that the stimulus has over the student's behavior/response. The instructor would then reinforce the student for saying "red," but would not have reinforced the student if he had said anything else. Once again, this is an example of the power of reinforcement. Reinforcing only "red" *teaches* and *manipulates* the behavior of the student, thus increasing the chances that the same behavior will happen again in the future when the same stimulus is presented.

Discrimination training consists of three phases of "trials" where DTT is used:

1. Mass Trial Phase; includes
   a. Isolation stage
   b. Distractor stage
   c. Block trial stage
2. Expanded Trial Phase
3. Random Rotation Phase (aka mixed trials)

The *mass trial* is the first phase and is a series of successive teaching trials that ensures successful learning on the part of the student. The mass trial phase begins with prompted trials (errorless learning) as the new stimulus is taught, and then the instructor systematically fades the prompts until the student responds independently. This occurs by utilizing the same instruction (S^D) each time and initially having only that stimulus present on the table (making it easy for the student to make the correct response). For example, the instructor says, "Give me the red one" five times in succession when only a red item is on the table. Then the instructor uses other *known* items as a "distractor," that is, placing a known item on the table with the target item (only two items on the table at one time), but still providing only the one instruction of "Give me the red one." Next, the instructor places an *unknown* item on the table as a distractor along with the target stimulus (only two items on the table at one time) for each trial. Finally, the instructor increases the number of items on the table to three, first using known and then unknown items. Before moving to the next phase, the student should be independently responding correctly at least 80% of the time.

When deciding which known and unknown distractor items to use, instructors should choose items that are maximally discriminable in terms of

- physical appearance (e.g., a block and a car),
- sound (e.g., "cup" vs. "dinosaur"), and
- function (e.g., a ball and truck vs. a shoe and sock).

For targets that do not involve the use of visible stimuli, different response topography should be used (e.g., hands vs. feet).

Each time a new skill area (i.e., nonverbal imitation, receptive identification of objects, performance of actions) is introduced, there will not yet be other known items to use as distractors. Thus, initially, only other mastered tasks and unknowns can be used. Once the first target item is taught using the mass trial phase, the entire phase should be repeated to teach a second target item before proceeding to the next phase. When the two target items (target #1 and target #2) have been taught in isolation, then the instructor performs *block trials* by beginning with either target #1 or target #2 and then presenting each in blocks of trials in the following manner:

1. Present a block of trials of target #1 in the presence of target #2 for approximately six trials. (Make sure at least the last two trials are independent correct responses before going to the next step.)
2. Give the student a brief break (i.e., a short play break).
3. Call the student back to the desk and present a block of trials of target #2 in the presence of target #1 for approximately six trials. As needed, prompt the correct response on the "switch trial" (i.e., when switching from one target to the other).
4. Decrease the number of trials per block.

5. Decrease the length of the break until both blocks are being conducted within the same sitting.
6. Fade the level of prompting on the switch trial.

The *expanded trial* is the phase of discrimination training in which the number of distractors that are presented between the instructions/S^Ds for the target stimulus/item are systematically increased. This phase is designed to build the student's memory retention. In the mass trial phase, there is a distractor item (if physical items are used) placed on the table near the target item to teach discrimination. Now, in the expanded trial phase, the instructor still has known and unknown distractor items on the table (if the target item is a physical object); however, *distractor trials* are presented between the target item trials. These distractor trials can be any other mastered/known instruction ("Do this", "Show me _____", "Give me _____"). At first, there is only one distractor trial between target trials with two distractors on the table; those distractors need to change and be moved around to different locations on the table for every new discrete trial (S^D–R–S^R). The same instruction is still used for each trial (e.g., "Give me the red one") during this phase. Gradually, the instructor increases the number of distractor trials between the target trial until there are approximately five to six trials between the target trials. Once the student has reached 80% or greater, independent accuracy for responding, it is time to move to the next phase.

At this stage (or any similar stage), if students are struggling with learning new target items or retaining the new target items that they appeared to have previously learned, instructors can use the strategy of *collapsing trials*. As was just presented for expanding trials, an instructor can use the same procedure to collapse the trials, such that there are not as many distractor trials presented between the target trials. This allows the student more opportunities (repetitions) to practice responding to the target trial and thus achieve greater success with learning. It is better for the student's successful learning to employ the strategy of collapsing trials than it is to repeatedly provide extensive prompting through multiple uses of the error correction procedure. Collapsing trials is another errorless learning strategy to ensure success and motivation with learning.

The *random rotation phase* is the phase where the instructor *randomly* mixes all the target responses together with other distractor trials in between. There should be no pattern to how often or when the different S^Ds are provided for the different target trials. This is to ensure that the student has truly learned to *discriminate* the different target items from each other, as well as from other instructions. If the target items are the ones placed on the table, then it is imperative that the instructor move the items around to different positions on the table at all times so that the student does not use the *location* of an item as a prompt. Once again, the student needs to achieve greater than 80% independent accuracy in responding.

Discrimination training is not truly finished until the student has demonstrated that he can generalize, maintain, and independently use the newly learned items throughout his everyday life. This means that once the student has learned "red," "blue," "yellow," "green," "orange," and so forth, the instructor then provides opportunities for the student to use the skill across people, environments, and other instructions and stimuli, with the parents also providing opportunities around the house and in the community. This means that *different*

- instructors, and other adults, need to be presenting the same instruction;
- items (or even items in books) that are "red" or "blue," and so on, are used;
- wording of instructions (e.g., "Where is the red one?," "Find the red one.") is used; and
- settings other than at the desk are used.

Promoting generalization also means using more natural wording with instructions, using reinforcers that are more natural to the current situation, using trials that are less "discrete" and more similar to typical interactions, and using "incidental" opportunities that arise during different and ongoing activities throughout the day. If a learner is able to correctly respond only when people use the exact same words under the exact same conditions, it is clear that additional work needs to be completed for the student to acquire functional command of the skill.

Note: The different types of data that are used during discrimination training are discussed in the section on data-based decision making.

☆ Practice Beginning Exercise

Each person needs to take the time to

- identify a skill that would typically be a target skill to teach, at some point, to a student with ASD;
- write out the materials needed and sequence of trials with S^Ds that will be used to teach the student the new skill, going through the three stages of the mass trial phase;
- write out the materials needed and sequence of trials and S^Ds that will be used when the student moves to the expanded trial phase for learning that skill;
- write out the materials needed and sequence of trials and S^Ds that will be used when the student moves to the random rotate phase; and
- describe different ways that the skill will be generalized and maintained.

☆ Practice Role-Play Scenario

Two people work together and practice teaching the new skills (the ones they just worked on in the beginning exercise) to each other. Take the time to note any changes that need to be made to the procedures as mistakes are identified during practice. Use the discrimination training evaluation/observation form provided in Appendix L.

☆ Quick Review

Discrimination training consists of three phases of "trials" in which DTT is used:

1. Mass Trial Phase, includes
   a. Isolation stage
   b. Distractor stage
   c. Block trial stage
2. Expanded Trial Phase
3. Random Rotation Phase (aka mixed trials)

Discrimination training is not completed until the student has generalized the skills across different scenarios and environments.

5 Assessing Students and Establishing an Overall DTT Program

ABA intervention programs are developed for implementation in one of several possible locations or environments. If a child receives an ASD diagnosis at a very young age (e.g., around 18 months), the program will often be implemented in the family's home, with the behavior analysts and therapists going to the home to implement the program. The program could also be implemented at an early intervention center, where there are therapy rooms where behavior analysts and other therapists work with the child. Many of these therapy rooms have a one-way mirror so parents or professionals can observe. Later, once the child has grown older, or if a child is diagnosed around the age of 3, the child's intervention program may still be implemented in the home or an early intervention center. Additionally, the child may now have the possibility of attending a preschool that has been specifically set up and designed as an ABA preschool for children with ASD. If the child attends a preschool, she will have an Individualized Family Service Plan (IFSP) in which the child's goals and objectives are written in a formal manner and the intervention plan to address those goals and objectives is explained. When a child reaches the age of 5 to 6, he will attend school; his parents can decide to send him to a private school, such as an ABA-emphasis school for children with ASD, or to a public school. Many public schools offer an ABA class for children with ASD. If the child has made good progress during the years spent in early intervention programs, it is possible that the child could attend a general education class, with paraeducator assistance and/or pullout special education services and/or an after-school in-home ABA program. Once a child starts attending a public elementary school, she will have an Individualized Education Program (IEP), which identifies goals and objectives, along with an explanation of the intervention and placement services that the child will receive. Early intervention is typically considered to go up through age 8, and ABA intervention programs implemented during this time period are often referred to as early intensive behavior intervention (EIBI).

Throughout the child's time spent in an ABA intervention program, he may also have a Behavior Support Plan (BSP). BSPs identify proactive/antecedent intervention strategies. Similarly, a student may have a Behavior Intervention Plan (BIP) that identifies proactive/antecedent and reactive/consequence intervention strategies that address the student's inappropriate behaviors that inhibit learning and/or functioning in a learning or community environment. This aspect of an ABA program is not discussed in the context of this book, but there are many resources for parents to help them understand ABA interventions for targeted inappropriate or problem behaviors. The BCBAs who are directing the overall ABA intervention program for the child have extensive training and experience in assessing a child's behavior and developing and implementing behavior change plans and strategies. Parents will need training to implement behavior change strategies in the home.

It is important to note that collaboration with parents is one of the most important components of a successful implementation of an ABA intervention program. ASD is an all-encompassing and mystifying disabling condition. While we know it is biological in nature and linked to genetic factors, we still do not know the exact cause or causes. Parents and professionals need to build trust and accountability with each other when treating a child with ASD using ABA. Honesty from both professionals and parents about the child's abilities and deficits, the progress or lack of progress the child makes during intervention, and how parents feel about the techniques being used are the foundation for a strong and cohesive team. Disagreements among and between parents and professionals should be seen as opportunities to work together in brainstorming and developing a better program overall for the student.

To establish an appropriate, effective, evidence-based, and functional ABA teaching program for a student with ASD, the individuals or teams of professionals and parents will need to

1. conduct a comprehensive skills assessment,
2. develop a profile of the student's abilities and deficits,
3. prioritize and decide on the skills and behaviors the student needs to acquire,
4. write a set of goals and objectives (e.g., an IEP) that addresses the student's deficits,
5. create and implement an education program to teach the new skills to the student,
6. use an appropriate data collection system for continued and consistent analysis of the student's progress and to implement changes to the overall program, and
7. ensure program implementation with treatment integrity through continued and consistent performance evaluation of ABA therapists working with a student with ASD.

Elements 1–5 in the list will be discussed in this chapter and elements 6 (data collection and analysis) and 7 (performance evaluation) will be discussed in the two subsequent chapters.

Because individuals with ASD often demonstrate splinter skills (high levels of ability in some areas and inconsistent or low ability levels in others), a comprehensive skills assessment allows the curriculum planning team to gain a clearer picture of what "holes" they need to address. Once the assessment is complete, a thorough profile of the student's skills can be developed, thus displaying to the team what critical skills the student needs to learn.

Taylor and McDonough (1996) outlined five questions that should be kept in mind when assessing a child's skills: (a) "Is the skill demonstrated upon your verbal instruction?"; (b) "Is the skill demonstrated without your assistance?"; (c) "Is the skill demonstrated reliably over time?"; (d) "Are all components of the skill demonstrated?"; and (e) "Is the skill demonstrated with several different people, in several different contexts, with various stimuli?" (p. 63). Each of these questions is addressed in the original *Assessment of Basic Language and Learning Skills: An Assessment, Curriculum Guide, and Skills Tracking System for Children with Autism or Other Developmental Disabilities* (ABLLS; Partington & Sundberg, 1998a). A newer *Assessment of Basic Language and Learning Skills–Revised* (ABLLS-R; Partington, 2006), as well as the *Verbal Behavior Milestones Assessment and Placement Program* (VB-MAPP; Sundberg, 2008a, 2008b), both are currently available. These criterion-referenced assessment tools are designed to assess a child's current skills; they also provide educators and parents with curricula that assist in identifying educational objectives. These tools assess a variety of language skills related to gauging a child's motivation to respond, ability to attend to a variety of stimuli (nonverbal and verbal), ability to generalize skills, and tendency to spontaneously use those skills (Partington & Sundberg, 1998a; Partington, 2006; Sundberg, 2008a, 2008b).

Both the ABLLS-R (Partington, 2006) and VB-MAPP (Sundberg, 2008a, 2008b) focus on categories of behavior across a variety of salient skills: (a) basic learner skills assessment (different skill sets, including cooperation and reinforcement effectiveness, receptive language, and social interaction); (b) academic skills assessment (different skill sets, including reading, math, and writing); (c) self-help skills assessment (different skill sets, including dressing, eating, and toileting); (d) motor skills assessment (gross motor and fine motor skills); and (e) group learning skills (small and large group). These types of assessments identify, for the intervention team, the skills and behaviors that the student needs to increase.

The VB-MAPP also provides a tool (Barriers Assessment) that enables the assessor to identify the primary learning and language barriers that are impeding the student's learning. This gives the intervention team a guide for completing necessary functional assessments (FAs) of individual target behaviors. Examples of barriers to learning are self-stimulation, hyperactivity, failure to generalize, scrolling, impaired imitation, weak motivators, prompt dependency, and lack of instructional control (Sundberg, 2008a). This assessment identifies the specific behaviors (barriers to learning—listed above) that need to be decreased for the student to successfully learn new skills that will be targeted in his IEP.

Once an assessment of skills has been completed, ABLLS-R and VB-MAPP provide a set of profile grids that allow the IEP team to transfer the scores from the assessment to the corresponding grids for each skill and gain a summary or overall picture of the student's strengths and deficits. As mentioned earlier, individuals with ASD display an unbalanced pattern of skill development. This is something that is unique to ASD, in that there are often holes or gaps and inconsistent learning patterns in an individual's skill set that can often be mystifying. For example, a student may be able to decode/read words, but be unable to identify the names of the letters that appear within the words; or a student may have an obsession with things being clean and in a certain order, but engage in the behavior of feces smearing. Still other students may be able to follow two- to three-step instructions, but have only three one-word items/activities that they request independently. This is why it is important to use a skills and behavior assessment that identifies the skills and deficits within the different skill areas, as well as across developmental milestones.

After the initial assessment, a report should be provided to parents to review prior to the in-home team, or IEP/IFSP, meeting. It should provide an overview of the skills assessment (known as the Milestones Skill Assessment) and the learning barriers and behavior characteristics (known as the Barriers Assessment). Copies of the resulting bar graphs (across Levels 1, 2, and 3) should also be created so that they can be given to and explained to the parents at the meeting.

There are other assessments that the ABA intervention team needs as well. The student should receive a speech and language assessment (along with a report), preferably conducted by a speech–language pathologist (SLP) who specializes in working with children with ASD. It is helpful if the SLP uses the echoic section of VB-MAPP for assessing the student's current language, communication, and vocal articulation skills. Additionally, more-specific speech and language assessments should be used to assess articulation skills in greater depth; more-advanced assessments of language skills, and/or augmentative and alternative communication needs, are required for children who are nonverbal. Another assessment that is helpful for the student's team to have is one completed by an occupational therapist (OT). Gaining an understanding of a student's abilities and deficits in gross and fine motor skills and possible sensory issues helps teams understand sensory challenges, such as hypersensitivity to certain stimuli (e.g., sounds), and what a student is able to do and not do when it comes to motor/physical activities. The combination of these assessments provides the team with a thorough overview of the student's motor, communication and language, and learning skill abilities and deficits.

When the team meets to discuss the assessments, they can decide whether it will be beneficial for the student to receive ongoing services from the SLP and

OT. Professionals in these fields who specialize in working with children with ASD and who have an understanding of ABA and possibly use some or all of the same techniques can make an immense difference and provide great benefit for children with ASD. Behavior analysts have training in language development, but generally not in working on articulation or utilizing a speech-generating device with a nonverbal child or designing and implementing motor skill development therapies.

Relative to including an SLP or OT as part of a student's overall intervention team, it is important to make sure that the intervention strategies these individuals use will not interfere with or counteract identified ABA methodology and intervention goals. For example, if the SLP or OT uses strategies where she always and only follows the child's lead, always allows the learner to do what he wants, and never provides compliance-enhancing instructions, this would act against the methodology and strategies used in ABA. ABA methods permit a balance between a child's motivation and need for adult-directed skill and behavior development. This same balance should apply to ancillary therapies, such as speech/language and OT. The parents of the child with ASD should always be asked to contribute information about their main concerns for their child and family, as well as their short- and long-term goals across the different skill areas. This greatly helps the program supervisor understand what the parents feel is most important for their child and their family. If the parents do not yet have an understanding of what is developmentally appropriate at particular stages in their child's life, it is the responsibility of the program supervisor to provide appropriate information about skill development.

The process of assessment and subsequently creating a student profile helps significantly in bringing together the ABA professionals and parents in deciding and agreeing upon the priority and order of skills to be targeted. To learn some skills, a person must first master other skills or behaviors as a foundation; then the person can work on learning a more advanced skill. It is important to keep in mind that some skills or behaviors will emerge or can be effectively taught during certain developmental stages and thus do not necessarily build on prerequisite skills.

Consider the case of a 5-year-old boy who is not toilet trained, does not eat more than four different foods, and is not yet sleeping for more than 4 hours a night. In this scenario, the parents may take the lead in prioritizing which skill/behavior the team will target first because of the effect it has on their family and home environment. All of the aforementioned self-help and adaptive behavior skills are developmentally appropriate for a 5-year-old. Since he has not yet gained any of these skills, and toileting is independent of sleeping, the prioritization of targeting one skill over another can be based on a combination of the student's needs and his family's priorities and preferences. At other times the parents of a 5-year-old child might ask a supervising behavior analyst to target reading. Assume in this case the child does not yet have a functional means of communication, nor does he sit to engage in instructional activities for more than 2 minutes. In this instance the behavior analyst would take the lead in prioritizing the skills to target prerequisites to reading. These developmentally appropriate targets would create a foundation for the student to later learn to read.

The final process of prioritizing a student's needs (and thus what will be the current focus of the ABA program) is for the behavior analyst to assist the team in deciding how many different skills (and behaviors) should be targeted at one time. This decision will depend on a number of factors, including

- the student's age;
- the number of intervention hours the student will be receiving per week;
- the nature and functionality of the target skills;
- how quickly the student learns new skills; and
- how much time will need to be focused on certain target behaviors, especially learning barriers.

All of the factors need to be considered, but some are more important at different stages of a program. Some variables carry more weight at the beginning of a new intervention program. In contrast, other factors are more important as the team evaluates the overall program each year and reprioritizes different skills and behaviors. These variables need to be individually considered for optimal outcomes. Final documents with goals and objectives are written in the manner appropriate for the location and type of service delivery (i.e., in-home, early intervention center, preschool, or school) and given to the parents for final review and approval. It is important that these documents be signed by all parties.

Once the goals and objectives have been approved by the planning team, the next step is to design and implement an ABA-based educational program that best meets the critical needs of the child. A checklist of critical program factors can be used to help a team create and put together an appropriate ABA-based educational program. An individualized and appropriate ABA-based educational program will address the following critical aspects:

- Is the program developmentally appropriate and age-appropriate for the child?
- Will the program help the child reduce problem behaviors and increase appropriate behaviors?
- Will the program allow teams to address the critical skill deficits of the child?
- Will the program allow teams to build on the strengths of the child?
- Does the program focus on the child's independent use of skills?
- Does the program consistently focus on skill generalization and maintenance across all the student's natural settings?

- Will the program allow the child to acquire skills within a reasonable amount of time?
- Does the program use a reliable data collection system to track the progress of the child's learning and the efficacy of the intervention program?

DTT is not the only appropriate ABA method of intervention to use when designing an overall ABA intervention program for students with ASD. Other ABA-based teaching methods are available and may be used along with DTT or as a next stage of intervention for a student. Some of these ABA-linked options include

- natural language paradigm (NLP),
- precision teaching,
- incidental teaching,
- fluency building,
- repeated practice,
- natural environment training (NET), and
- video modeling.

Most, but not all, individuals with ASD are visual learners with deficits in auditory processing. Consequently, there should be a strong emphasis on using visually based materials during teaching, such as picture and video stimuli, written text, and other visual teaching aids. As a result of their auditory processing deficits, many students with ASD have poorly developed receptive language, not only resulting in a need for visual orientation, but also requiring modification of language used during instruction. These factors need to be considered in developing an individualized ABA intervention program for each student. For some more advanced learners, there are several research-based cognitive behavior therapy (CBT) intervention strategies that are very effective with students with ASD. These methods, such as those that assist with social thinking and self-management, can be especially helpful for learners with ASD who receive some or all of their education in a general education setting.

Students with ASD who have been assessed using the VB-MAPP can be placed into one of three different levels based on the outcomes of their initial and sequential annual assessments. These learner levels can further be broken into four different elements to help the intervention team decide upon the type and delivery of the student's intervention program. These elements are the

- severity of the disabling condition,
- phase of development in which the student falls,
- amount of support a student needs to learn and progress (e.g., amount and type of resources needed, amount and type of environmental restrictions, how small skills/tasks need to be broken down), and
- teaching methods that are most effectively used when working on skills and behaviors with individual learners.

These elements can be correlated and combined, as shown in Table 4. During early intervention, a student's individualized intervention program can be based on these four different aspects within each learner level. These learner levels are discussed in greater detail below.

Based on their specialized training and education, behavior analysts are able to develop individualized intervention programs that follow a verbal behavior structure. A behavior analyst addresses these verbal behavior skills via development of teaching programs for each skill. All of the verbal behavior programs together make up an overall curriculum that follows the scope and sequence of skill development and milestones, such as those identified by the VB-MAPP. The VB-MAPP skills are arranged into 16 different milestone areas:

- mands (requesting);
- tacts (expressive labeling and commenting);

Table 4. Levels of Learning and Descriptive Elements in the *Verbal Behavior Milestones Assessment and Placement Program*[a]

Descriptive element	Level of learning		
	Level 1 – early learner	Level 2 – intermediate learner	Level 3 – advanced learner
Severity of disability	Severe learning barriers and slow acquisition	Moderate learning barriers and steady acquisition	Mild learning barriers and fast acquisition
Phase of development	Learning to learn	Building core language and learning skills	Preparing for school
Support needed	Extra support required	Medium support required	Minimal support required
Teaching methods utilized	Mostly 1:1 teaching, intensive DTT, intensive focus on learning barriers	1:1 teaching, DTT, some 1:2 (small group), NET, NLP, incidental teaching, parallel focus on learning barriers	Fading 1:1 teaching, some DTT, mostly small group teaching, NET, incidental teaching, NLP, CBT strategies, parallel focus on learning behaviors

Note. DTT = discrete trial training; NET = natural environment training; NLP = natural language paradigm; CBT = cognitive behavior therapy.

[a]VB-MAPP; Sundberg, 2008.

- intraverbal (responding to questions and fill-in-the-gap details);
- echoic (imitation of verbal skills);
- motor imitation;
- reading;
- writing;
- listener responding;
- listener responding by feature, function, and class (LRFFC);
- visual perceptual skills and matching to sample (VPMS);
- independent play;
- social behavior and social play;
- spontaneous vocal behavior;
- classroom routines and group skills;
- linguistic structure; and
- math.

As mentioned previously, the VB-MAPP is used both as an assessment tool and as a guide for scope and sequence of skill development and task analysis for goals and curriculum planning. A detailed description of each milestone area can be found in the VB-MAPP Guidebook. The sequence of progression within each skill area is outlined within the Task Analysis and Skills Tracking forms for each learner level (1, 2, and 3).

The first section of the VB-MAPP is the Milestones and Skills Tracking Assessment. This identifies verbal behavior milestones and related skills across three developmental levels:

Level 1 (0–18 months): Skills focus on basic learning-to-learn skills such as attending to others, sitting in a chair, following basic instructions, and making simple requests. These skills are the building blocks or foundation for all other learning.

Level 2 (18–30 months): Skills focus on expansion of and building strong core language and learning skills, including labeling items, following complex instructions, working in a group setting, and complex language skills such as asking and answering questions.

Level 3 (30–48 months): Skills focus on preparing for school, moving toward more academic tasks such as reading, writing, and math, while also continuing to expand Level 2 skills.

Almost all of the milestones follow a sequence across all learner levels and often overlap down through the scope of skills that are targeted in each learner level. This ensures that skills needed within different contexts are generalized and mastery is ensured within all areas the skills are needed.

Level 1 Learner – Learning to Learn

Students in the learning-to-learn development phase have yet to acquire the skills they need to learn skills from their environment. These students typically have moderate to severe learning barriers and can be slow at acquiring new skills. One primary focus of intervention at this level is reducing the student's most significant learning barriers. When working with students whose scores fall primarily in Level 1, the teaching team shapes the students' behaviors so that they can learn

- the basics of communicating their wants and needs (mands, echoics, vocal behavior, and tacts),
- how to behave appropriately in an educational setting so that they can respond to instruction (listener responding, imitation, behavior-learning barriers), and
- how to participate/behave appropriately (and find enjoyment) in motivating activities with peers and adults (social behavior, independent and social play).

These learners need *intensive* and *direct* skill intervention programs. This means that teaching should occur

- for a minimum of 5 hours a day (25 hours a week), Monday to Friday (but preferably 30–40 hours a week, including weekends);
- in a carefully organized and planned environment (minimizing distractions);
- with careful task analysis and incremental targets for skill acquisition;
- utilizing primarily DTT (structured) teaching sessions; and
- utilizing natural environment training (NET) to teach daily and functional living skills and routines incidentally across the student's day.

Throughout the day, students at this level also need to be continually working on motor skills, self-help skills, toileting, and social interaction skills.

Level 2 Learner – Building Core Language and Learning

Students who are working on Level 2 skills are beginning to show some solid language and learning skills and their acquisition rate is steady, and the need to minimize distractions in the environment has lessened. The focus of intervention is now on expanding their language and learning skills. In this level, the focus is on

- expanding vocabulary by teaching more nouns, verbs, and adjectives;
- increasing skills to respond to longer and multiple-step instructions;

- starting to work on identifying and sorting nouns/pictures by features, functions, and class;
- beginning intraverbal training (i.e., providing a response to an instruction that is open-ended and without the presence of specific materials that prompt the student's answer);
- developing social and expressive interactions with peers;
- developing group skills and following classroom routines independently;
- beginning to generalize skills to less intensive teaching settings;
- beginning to learn new skills within less intensive teaching methods (mass trial to trial by trial); and
- decreasing behaviors that continue to be moderate to significant learning barriers for the student.

It is important for Level 2 learners to become more independent in performing and utilizing their skills. It is also important that rote learning and prompt dependency are not occurring and becoming a learning barrier for the student.

Level 3 Learner – Preparing for School

Level 3 learners should no longer require high amounts of support and intensive teaching methods to behave appropriately and learn within a variety of 1:1 and small group learning activities. Learners should be acquiring new vocabulary easily and without formal teaching and should be able to sit for up to 20 minutes doing learning tasks (using a token economy system) without needing a break away from the desk. The focus of intervention for Level 3 learners should be on

- expanding conversation skills (linguistic structure, length of utterances, use of vocabulary, and variety of topics);
- asking questions for information;
- talking about things that are not present (intraverbals);
- developing beginning academic skills for reading, writing, and math;
- increasing the complexity of social interactions and play skills with peers;
- increasing the amount of time spent in group learning and group activities; and
- increasing the amount of incidental learning that takes place during naturally occurring daily routines and activities.

These learners are also continuing to develop their independence with self-help, communication, and motor skills, while reducing learning barriers to a minimum in order to participate in more activities in the community. For the few students in Level 3 who have reached kindergarten-level language, reading, and math skills, the program supervisor can begin to use the research-based teaching methodology of direct instruction and the curriculum produced by SRA/McGraw Hill: *Language for Learning, Reading Mastery,* and *Connecting Math Concepts.* All staff need to be trained in using this method of teaching. As a student approaches achievement of the Level 3 learner skills, the intervention or IFSP/IEP team begins their search for a new and less restrictive educational environment to which the student can transition and continue her education.

Conclusions

Individual programs/lesson plans (along with corresponding data sheets) need to be created and modified, as needed, at each learner level for each individual student. These should be stored in a student's electronic file and printed and placed in a binder for that student. This student program binder is maintained by the program supervisor and always contains all the current programs (and data sheets) that the student is working on. This student binder is used while instructors work with the student and is referred to when student progress and next steps for certain programs are reviewed. Shown in Appendix M are two examples of procedure sheets that can be used during the course of a student's intervention program. The data sheets discussed in the next chapter and provided in Appendix N correlate with these procedure sheets. This provides an overall picture of program development, with a procedure sheet and data sheet for each goal/target skill.

Many resources are available to guide program supervisors in choosing and creating appropriate curriculum and procedure sheets for the DTT program they are developing. These resources include *A Complete ABA Curriculum for Individuals on the Autism Spectrum with a Developmental Age of 1–4 Years* (Knapp & Turnbull, 2014; also one for developmental ages 3–5 and age 7 up to adulthood); *A Work in Progress: Behavior Management Strategies and a Curriculum for Intensive Behavioral Treatment of Autism* (Leaf & McEachin, 1999); *Behavioral Intervention for Young Children with Autism: A Manual for Parents and Professionals* (Maurice, Green, & Luce, 1996); and *Teaching Language to Children with Autism or Other Developmental Disabilities* (Partington & Sundberg, 1998b).

6 Data-Based Decision Making

Reliable and ongoing DTT data collection is essential for making effective decisions regarding a student's educational program. Indeed, having a data-based decision-making process to analyze and change students' programs and assist in-home and IFSP/IEP teams in ensuring that students are receiving an individualized and appropriate educational program is mandatory. No two students respond in the same manner to a DTT program, and, therefore, only through data collection, analysis, and interpretation can a program supervisor and an intervention team understand a student's learning process. Brief and basic explanations of the purpose of data collection, types of data, monitoring and analyzing data, the selection and creation of data sheets, summarizing data, data analysis and interpretation, and using data to make decisions are provided in this section.

Purpose of Data Collection

Data collection needs to be used in all areas of a student's ABA intervention program. It is recommended that a data collection system meet the following criteria for the skills to be measured:

1. It should be specific; it clearly defines the behaviors or skills to be measured.
2. It should be valid; it actually measures what it claims to measure.
3. It should be reliable; it remains consistent across observers.

If these three criteria are achieved, an intervention team will be able to use the data successfully for the following purposes:

- to understand how a student is progressing with each skill;
- to communicate to others at what level a student is performing;
- to demonstrate a student's mastery, generalization, and maintenance of skills;
- to improve the instructor's ability to provide optimal instruction; and
- to continue to provide an appropriate educational program.

Types of Data

The types of data collected will depend on the type of information that is needed to monitor progress and inform changes within a student's educational program. An IEP team, or an instructor, will collect data that informs them about how a student is learning a particular skill. Relative to students with ASD, specifically during the early learning stages, no *new* learning targets are introduced to a student unless mastery of the current target has been achieved or reevaluated. Mastery is individually determined, and the default mastery criterion of 80–100% correct across two to three separate instructors over 2–3 consecutive days is generally applied.

Data collection regarding skill performance is taken on the individual steps needed to gain skill mastery. Reaching mastery follows the three levels of teaching and data collection (and each level may involve different steps). This is all done to ensure the end result of independence with skill performance. The three levels are

> *Level 1*: Discrimination Training/Mass Trial (Acquisition)
>
> *Level 2*: Trial by Trial (Fluency and Generalization)
>
> *Level 3*: Cold Probe/First Trial Data (Independence and Maintenance)

Level 1

Level 1 is the acquisition stage of gaining a new skill and involves the most intensive teaching and data collection. This stage is accomplished by using discrimination training to teach the student how to discriminate and identify specific items when they are labeled. When discrimination training is being done, a mass trial data sheet is used. The four steps used in Level 1 are as follows:

> *Step 1:* Mass trials (providing the same instruction/S^D—for example, "Give me cat"—for 5–10 trials in sequence) are performed with the target item or action used in isolation until predetermined mastery is reached. Data is collected on every trial.
>
> *Step 2:* Mass trials are performed with the target item or action interspersed with the presentation of other known items or actions until predetermined mastery is achieved. Data is collected only on the target item or action.
>
> *Step 3:* Mass trials are performed with the target item or action interspersed with the presentation of unknown items or actions until predetermined mastery is achieved. Data is collected only on the target item or action.

Step 4: The target item or action is put into random rotation of presentation with other mastered items or actions in that same category until predetermined mastery is achieved. Data is collected only on the target item or action.

Within Level 1 (acquisition), data are monitored daily, and if a student is failing to meet his mastery criteria, the data are analyzed to determine why and action is taken to assist the student to meet those criteria. These alterations may include, but are not limited to,

- changing stimuli,
- changing the method of presentation of stimuli,
- changing error correction procedures,
- increasing the level or type of reinforcement,
- analyzing tasks and adding steps to simplify the task,
- reviewing whether the target was at an appropriate level for the student, and
- reviewing changes in environments.

These changes are communicated to the teaching team via e-mail or by team meeting, whichever will allow for the most immediate implementation.

Level 2

Level 2 is the stage at which instructors are trying to increase the student's fluency (rate of responding) while also generalizing the newly learned skills across different settings, items, and instructors or peers. A trial-by-trial data sheet is used to collect data on this skill as it is practiced across the day. Typically, there is a predetermined number of times the skill needs to be practiced throughout the day.

Within Level 2, the data are monitored daily or weekly, and if a student is not increasing in her fluency with performance of the skill or generalizing the skill across settings, the data are analyzed to determine why and action is taken to assist the student to meet those criteria. Lack of progress at this stage can often occur because of

- a lack of consistent presentation of instructions by different instructors,
- a low number of opportunities provided by the instructors for the student to perform the skill,
- inadvertent prompting made by an instructor, or
- a lack of motivation for the student to perform the skill.

Different instructors on the teaching team typically need to be observed working with the student (directly or through video clips taken) by the behavior analyst/supervisor of the teaching team to determine the specific reason for the student's lack of progress. Changes need to be communicated to the teaching team via e-mail or by team meeting, whichever will allow for the most immediate implementation.

Level 3

Level 3 is the stage at which the focus is on withholding any and all prompting and requiring the student to demonstrate (generalize) the skill independently at any time during the day. Skills in this level are typically performed in a small group, and incidental opportunities are provided through 1:1 teaching and play settings. Cold-probe/first-trial data are the only data collected to ensure that, at the first opportunity that was provided to the student to perform the skill, he performed it independently. This data is collected at first on a daily basis, then weekly and monthly and so on, as needed, to ensure continued independent use and maintenance of the skill. If the student is not maintaining the skill or has begun to require some prompting to perform the skill, the same analysis process as used in Level 2 is implemented. Changes are communicated to the teaching team via e-mail or at the weekly team meeting, whichever will allow for the most immediate implementation.

There are other types of data that are also frequently used when working with students in an ABA-supported educational setting, wherein DTT is used in formal and more natural settings to teach and track progress of skills. Below is a list of these additional types of data, with a brief description of each:

Proficiency or rate data. Data are collected to record how often, in a given amount of time, the student performs a behavior. These data are useful for skills that occur at a low rate or during a specified time period (e.g., the student initiated conversation seven times in a 20-minute free play session).

Duration data. These data measure how long a behavior lasts. They are useful for documenting challenging behavior (e.g., tantrums) and skills that need to last for a certain amount of time to be considered functional (e.g., the student independently engaged with art materials for 5 minutes).

Latency data. Latency data measure the length of time between the presentation of an instruction and the performance of the behavior or initiation of the behavior sequence (e.g., an instructor says, "Get your pencil" and then records the length of time that passes before the student retrieves his pencil). This type of data is often taken when the team is working on fluency with the student's responding.

Level-of-assistance data. These data reflect how much help or what type of prompting a student requires to perform a behavior or task. These are useful for chained tasks that cannot be described as correct or incorrect (e.g., the student required partial physical prompt to begin to follow the direction "Put it on the shelf," direct verbal prompt to turn on the water to begin a hand-washing routine, and a gestural prompt to use the soap).

Work sample data. These data are products of a student's performance related to a target skill. Work samples (e.g., a videotape of a social interaction, a photograph of a block tower built by the student, a copy of a drawing) provide a snapshot of current progress and are useful for skills that are difficult to capture with a checklist or data sheet.

Level of participation data. These data reflect how engaged the student was during the activity. This is typically measured with a rubric scoring system to indicate how much the student participated in the activity. This can include prompting and independence levels as well.

Selection and Creation of Data Sheets

There are many published and available data sheets suitable for use in DTT programs. However, because each student's program is individualized, data sheets will often need to be created to measure student progress on specific programs. Whether selecting an existing form or creating a new one, program supervisors are advised to address the following questions regarding the specific program and the skill or task being taught. Answers to these questions will assist in identifying the type of data sheet needed:

- Is the emphasis of the program on teaching a new skill or changing how the current one is being taught? *Example:* Is the team just starting to teach colors, or have they discovered that they need to change the method they were using to teach colors?
- What type of data will answer posed questions? The type of data collected will greatly narrow the type of data sheets that should or can be used. *Example:* Does the team need to take data that are + (occurrence) or − (no occurrence), or are they making tally marks on the occurrence of a behavior during a specified period of time?

- Will this type of data help address the goal/objective related to a particular skill? Program supervisors need to match closely the type of data collected to the language and skill of the objective to make sure that the information gained from the data sheet will enable changes to be made that will produce progress toward achieving the objective. *Example:* If a student is working on a goal to identify numbers 1 through 10, the intervention team will want to take data that allow them to know what percentage of the time when the student sees a 1 he correctly identifies it as 1; *and* if he is receptively or expressively identifying 1; *and* with how many other numbers presented in the display.
- If the student is in a classroom, will this data collection format fit into the classroom activities? Program supervisors need to make sure that the data collection sheets are organized so that they are understandable to paraprofessionals, instructional assistants, teachers, and other instructors and will be easy to read and use while interacting with and teaching the student. Instructors need to take the time to share and discuss the data sheets with the student's instructional team before beginning to use them. *Example:* If it is a busy classroom with more than a one-to-one adult-to-student ratio, the data sheets need to be simple, with large spaces and lettering, and designed to take the instructor only a second to write down a data point in the correct location.
- How will the data be summarized? The design of the data sheet and the type of data should make it easy to follow the progress of the student; it should be well organized, with appropriate sections for information at a glance. *Example:* Because most data will ultimately be summarized in a graph, a data sheet needs to have the student's name, the skill being taught, the date of each time data was taken, and a field for the data points.
- Is the data collection format simple enough and easy to use for everyone taking data in the different environments? It is important that the data to be taken match the level and expertise of the individuals who are being asked to collect them. Many individuals who are not behavior analysts or trained ABA therapists will not collect data if it is difficult to understand, hard to do, unclear relative to its purpose, or overly labor intensive. This means prioritizing the data that is most needed and keeping in mind that the quality of data collected is more important than the quantity.
- How will the data be analyzed? Before too much data are taken with a new data sheet, the sheet should be tested to see how the data will be summarized and analyzed. *Example:* Once data have been collected for a couple of days on a given skill, the classroom teacher should graph the

data and see if she is able to analyze the data and determine some pattern of learning that is occurring; if not, she may need to pick or design a different type of data sheet to use for that skill.

Each data sheet designed to measure a specific skill should accompany the procedure sheet for that specific skill. At the top of each data sheet there should be a brief summary (taken from the detailed procedure sheet) of the criteria and procedures. It is recommended that the following information appear at the top of each data sheet:

- same title as the procedure sheet, with the student's name;
- type of data/trial (e.g., mass trial, cold probe);
- mastery criteria;
- error correction procedure;
- ratio of reinforcement to use;
- S^Ds to be used based on level;
- required response of the student; and
- levels/steps that instructors will follow.

Two examples of data sheets as described above are provided in Appendix N. These data sheets correspond to the procedure sheets provided in Appendix M so that the reader can see how a procedure sheet and data sheet are made to accompany each other.

Progress Monitoring and Data Analysis

Ongoing objective data collection allows for consistent and continuous assessment, monitoring, and recording of student performance across time. Typically there are different tiers of data monitoring and analysis that occur within an in-home, center-based, or school intervention team. The tiers refer to the frequency of monitoring and analysis, as well as to the individual responsible within tiers/levels for making data-based decisions. Each organization or school that is providing ABA intervention services will have their own tiers of monitoring, and strategies and protocol for analyzing data. This author has typically created four different tiers of staff that are responsible for different aspects of data monitoring for each student or within a classroom. These tiers are based on the level of expertise that the person has in analyzing data and determining what data are telling team members about student learning and/or behavior.

Tier 1: The first person responsible for data review is the therapist/instructor (typically a paraeducator, an ABA therapist, or a registered behavior technician [RBT]) who is directly working with the student at the point of performance of the skill or behavior. Current performance levels are checked against recent per-formance and significant variation is identified and analyzed by senior therapists (e.g., an experienced RBT, a BCaBA, or a classroom teacher); immediate action is taken if needed. This person also records on the data sheet if mastery for a certain skill has occurred and registers this data on the program sheet with the date of mastery. This means that the next instructor who works with the student needs to note this progress report and introduce the next skill or level, also recording the date for beginning that skill/level. Initials of instructors recording the data are also written next to the data, on the data sheet, so that, if needed, future dis-cussions about the data can occur with that person.

Tier 2: The second person responsible for data review is the senior therapist (e.g., an experienced RBT, a BCaBA, or a classroom teacher), who at the end of the day or at specific times during the week reviews student progress and deals with questions and issues that instructors/therapists have identified. If the se-nior therapist finds a problem that she is unable to make a decision about alone, that matter will be discussed with the clinical/program supervisor (BCBA, SLP, or other qualified personnel) as soon as possible. The senior therapist is also responsible for letting the program/clinical supervisor know when all the levels of a specific program or behavior performance for a student have been mastered and a new program with procedure sheet and/or data sheet is needed.

Tier 3: The third tier involves the professionals responsible for writing the goals and objectives for students. This includes the clinical/program supervisor (BCBA), SLP, OT, and so on. These professionals must spend a certain amount of time per week or month with the student to maintain an overall understand-ing of the student's learning style and skill acquisition rate and his strengths and deficits. It is also important that this person maintain instructional control with the student and thus periodically directly work with the student to experi-ment with different teaching strategies and identify and write new procedures for teaching a skill. It is also important that this person work periodically with the student so that she can ensure that the student is demonstrating independence (not becoming overly prompt-dependent) and that skill generalization and main-tenance are on course. This professional also needs to meet regularly with the senior therapist and the whole team so that they can collectively discuss student progress. These meetings are essential for discussing data and new or modified teaching procedures. This professional also regularly observes, either via video or in person, the therapists, teacher, and so forth who work with the student. These regularly scheduled observations allow supervisors to provide informed feedback regarding other instructors' adherence to teaching procedures and their compe-tency with the DTT and other teaching methods.

Tier 4: The fourth tier is the clinical director (ideally an experienced BCBA or a BCBA-D—a Board Certified Behavior Analyst with a doctorate), who supervises clinical/program supervisors within the organization or school. This professional will typically not work directly with students, but rather meet regularly with the clinical/program supervisors to review and provide advice about teaching procedures, data collection and analysis, and progress of individual students. This professional is also available to the clinical/program supervisors when they encounter particular difficulties, such as with a student's program or behavior, with the student's parents, or management difficulties with instructors on the team. This professional also typically provides ongoing professional development for the clinical/program supervisors and may also be a part of the training that is provided to new ABA therapists or RBTs.

Figure 3 shows a diagram that outlines how the ABA professionals listed above can implement ongoing recording, monitoring, and analysis of student performance and program progress. While this process is recommended, it is important to keep in mind that each organization or school will have individualized data collection, monitoring, and analysis processes and procedures.

After a student's initial assessment and the team/IEP/IFSP meeting occurs, there is an ongoing process of assessment, monitoring, and recording of student performance. Overlap among personnel involved in this process, including the reporting of student achievement within the different tiers of ABA professionals discussed above, is an essential check-and-balance element. It is important to note that daily data collection on each student's targeted goals and objectives is the most intensive, crucial, and all-encompassing process. All other methods follow this salient data element.

1. Daily Data Collection
   a. Every day, throughout the day, detailed data are collected on each student's skills for each goal and objective.
      i. A separate and individualized data collection sheet is used for each teaching program. The sheet is kept in the student's binder or on a clipboard that belongs only to that student.
      ii. Data are collected immediately while teaching is occurring so that they are guaranteed to be accurate.
   b. All data sheets are reviewed daily for student mastery (or lack of mastery), and new levels or skills are introduced immediately once mastery is reached.
2. Weekly Progress Monitoring
   a. Each week the following data review and progress monitoring meetings occur:
      i. The senior therapist/classroom teacher, the clinical supervisor, and the SLP meet separately or together to review data and discuss the student's individual program progress.

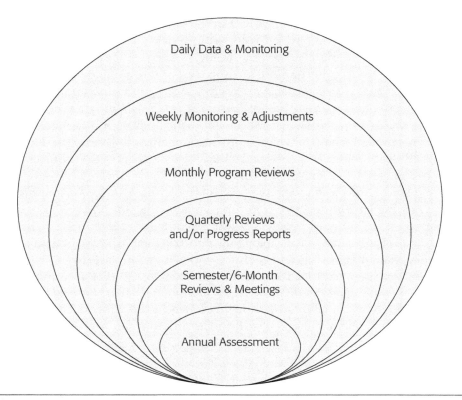

Daily Data & Monitoring

Weekly Monitoring & Adjustments

Monthly Program Reviews

Quarterly Reviews
and/or Progress Reports

Semester/6-Month
Reviews & Meetings

Annual Assessment

Figure 3. How applied behavior analysis (ABA) professionals can implement on-going recording, monitoring, and analysis of student performance and program progress.

    ii. In-home/class team meetings occur on a specified day each week. Any changes that are occurring related to individual student programs are discussed and explained.

b. Each week or every 2 weeks, the program/clinical supervisor spends time with the student and intervention team to observe, coach, take intensive data, and/or experiment with new teaching and management strategies.

c. Each week, previously specified data are charted on a graph or entered into individualized Excel spreadsheets. Graphs are automatically updated to show daily progress or lack of progress. The clinical team use these data to make changes to teaching and intervention plans, as needed.

    d. Each week, programs for each student are discontinued, amended, or continued based on the student's challenges or progress.

    e. Each week, the clinical director, clinical/program supervisors, and classroom teachers/senior therapists communicate with each other and with parents regarding any issues that have arisen and input that is needed from the home or clinical team regarding ongoing programs and so forth.

3. Monthly Program Reviews

    a. Each month, a brief monthly program summary (two to three pages) is completed. This document is given to the clinical director, parents, and all members of the intervention team. It summarizes the progress on the student' goals, with small graphs, if applicable, and changes that have been made throughout the past several weeks. If the student's program is implemented at a school or center, it can also be helpful for the parents to receive short videos stored on a USB that show learners working, along with a copy of the program summary. These videos allow parents to see examples of student engagement in learning activities through the month that correspond to individual goals and objectives.

    b. Team meetings for all members of the intervention team occur monthly. These important meetings are often the only time everyone is together; hence, they are vital. The clinical/program supervisor leads this meeting (often reviewing the program summary) and typically does training on new teaching and/or behavior intervention procedures.

4. Quarterly Reviews and/or IEP Progress Monitoring

    a. Four times a year, the daily data on students' goals and objectives are used to create a comprehensive progress report. This is often an IEP/IFSP Progress Report, designed to provide the clinical director and parents with a report on each learner's annual goal and objective progress. For in-home and center-based programs for very young children, this step may be skipped if the information is redundant to the monthly program summaries and 6-month progress reports.

5. 6-month or Semester IEP Progress Reports

    a. Halfway through the year, students undergo a reassessment using the VB-MAPP or ABLLS-R. This allows the program/clinical supervisor to review each student's progress in detail and to change specific goals and objectives, as needed.

    b. A meeting is held with the parents to go through a formal review of each student's progress relative to goals and objectives.

    c. An IEP/IFSP Progress Report (for preschools and schools) or Progress Report (for in-home and centers) is given to the parents within 2–3 weeks after the progress review meeting; a parent signature is typically required.

6. Annual Assessment

    a. The process that is described at the beginning of the chapter "Assessing Students and Establishing an Overall DTT Program" is repeated.

       i. A VB-MAPP or ABLLS-R assessment update is performed, and the results are recorded and reviewed (this review process often includes participation of the clinical director).

       ii. This information is provided to the parents prior to the meeting.

       iii. A team meeting is held with the parents to discuss progress and reprioritize the skills and behaviors that will be targeted for acquisition and improvement.

       iv. A document with the new set of annual goals and objectives is written, and all parties sign it and agree to its implementation.

Note: Behavior Support Plans (BSP) and/or Behavior Intervention Plans (BIP) are also discussed at annual review meetings. Procedures for data collection and a new report written to describe student progress, along with any new proactive or reactive procedures that are needed, are included. Parent signatures are required and acquired following program review and agreements.

Summarizing Data

Summarizing data is a crucial part of determining the success of a student's DTT program. It is through the summary of data that the program/clinical supervisors and the intervention team will be able to look at an overall picture (over time), locate patterns of acquisition, and determine whether suitable progress is being made. The goal of summarizing data is to display the progress a student is making in learning a specific skill, as well as to determine the student's unique learning patterns.

The manner in which data are summarized will depend on the type of data collected. Graphing is one of the most efficient and comprehensive ways to summarize and display data and is suitable for the following types of data: frequency/accuracy, trial by trial, random rotation, level of assistance, rate, duration, and cold probe/first trial. Figure 4 provides examples of frequency/accuracy, rate, and duration data graphs.

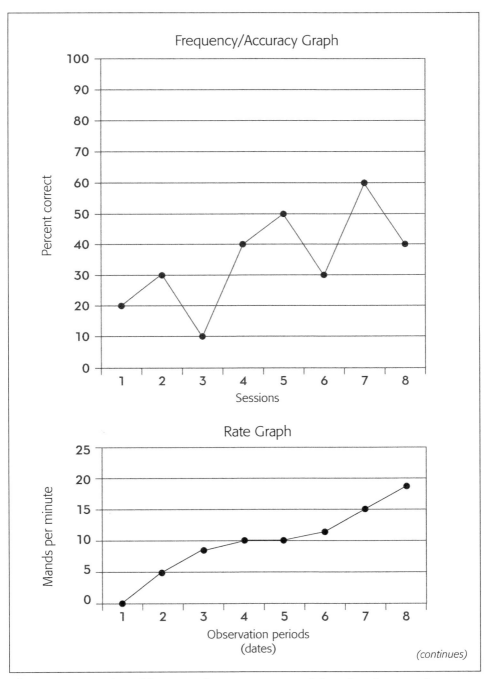

Figure 4. Examples of frequency/accuracy, rate, and duration data graphs.

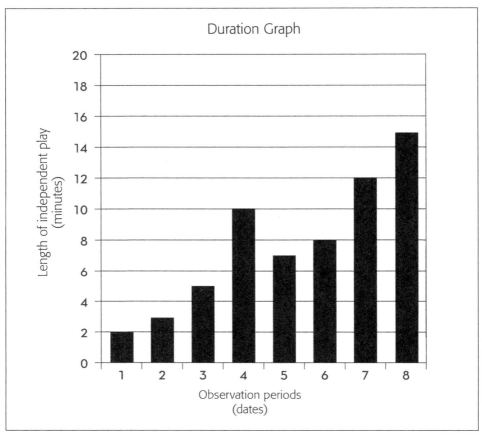

Figure 4. (*continued*)

Data Analysis and Interpretation

There are different ways to analyze data. Data can be analyzed by looking for patterns of progress or lack of progress; patterns that occur with prompting, incorrect responses, or mastery of skills are also considered. These analyses and interpretations are typically done as a part of day-to-day and weekly progress monitoring. Another way of doing data analysis is to use a blank graph or celebration chart, with titles already filled in. Instructors manually fill in a student's achievements on these standardized forms. Then, after a few days or weeks, a picture of the student's overall progress provides the instructors and clinical/program supervisor valuable information about the student's overall progress or lack of progress.

As mentioned previously, senior therapists (or others) can set aside time weekly to enter the data into an Excel spreadsheet that produces a graph, and then review that graph weekly. In this fashion, the actual interpretation and analysis follows the same protocol as described for manual graphing. There are also software programs that allow instructors to enter data during instruction, with graphing occurring simultaneously with data entry.

By studying a graph, the clinical/program supervisor can answer the question of whether the instructional procedures are working and determine whether the student is progressing and what patterns of learning are occurring. The goal is to provide the best instruction by eliminating ineffective teaching and interventions and implementing methods that prove to be effective. Summarizing and analyzing data needs to occur frequently so necessary instructional changes can be made as early as possible.

The key component of data analysis is determining not only whether a student is progressing, but also whether specific patterns are occurring that are assisting the student in or impeding him from learning new skills. In addition, it is important to understand the problem-solving process that data analysis and interpretation involve. Typically, there is no single reason for the results that the data display. The instructor will use the data to help the team determine a course of action with the understanding that they are engaging in hypothesis testing (e.g., "We believe that the data suggest that John is not learning [skill] because [reason]; therefore, we will now try to do [new procedures]"). If that plan works, the hypothesis was correct; if it does not, another hypothesis will need to be developed and another course of action taken.

☆ Practice Data Analysis and Interpretation

Refer to the graphs in Figure 5 and attempt to determine (a) whether the student is progressing, (b) what might be impeding or assisting acquisition of the skill, and (c) what suggestions you might give the IEP team and the instructor regarding future work on this skill. This exercise will be most beneficial if you attempt to analyze the data independently before reading the suggested analysis provided below each graph.

Using Data to Make Decisions

The significant amount of individual attention given to data collection and analysis, including the expertise of experienced ABA professionals on students' intervention teams, is one of the important elements of ABA that make it different and set it above other intervention methods. The monitoring and analysis of what is

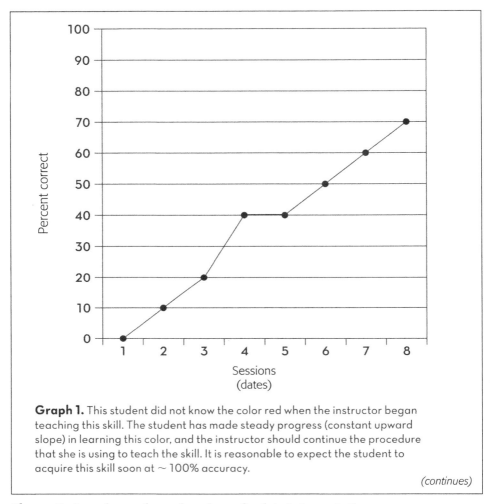

Graph 1. This student did not know the color red when the instructor began teaching this skill. The student has made steady progress (constant upward slope) in learning this color, and the instructor should continue the procedure that she is using to teach the skill. It is reasonable to expect the student to acquire this skill soon at ~ 100% accuracy.

(continues)

Figure 5. Sample graphs and analyses for data interpretation.

actually happening is much different and more effective than what people *think* is happening. Data provide factual documents, and the importance of using factual records to monitor student programs cannot be overstated.

Decisions made based on data and not on a gut feeling or general observation mean that details and the student's step-by-step progress or lack of progress are consistently monitored, and immediate and informed changes can be made if there are difficulties.

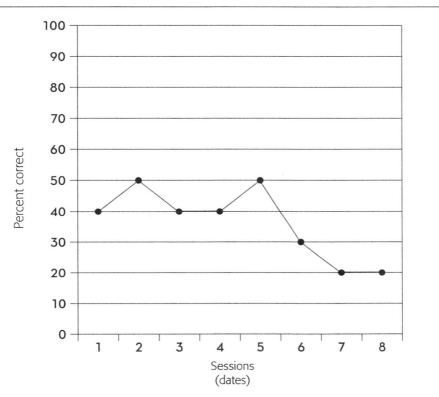

Graph 2. This student was able to identify the color red some of the time when the instructor began teaching this skill. For a while, the student maintained approximately the same level of ability (no downward or upward slope), and then he began to steadily lose the skill of identifying red (constant downward slope). The instructor should not continue using the procedure that he is using to teach the skill. It is reasonable to expect that if the instructor does not change the teaching procedure, the student will completely lose the ability to identify red and may have difficulty learning to identify colors in the future. Possible reasons for this loss of skill: (a) instructor does not have appropriate instructional control, (b) instructor is not providing appropriate reinforcement when the student does provide the correct answer, (c) the instructor is not providing enough or the right type of prompt to teach the student what "red" is, (d) the instructor is not ensuring that the student is attending before providing instruction, (e) the instructor is not using the correction procedure when the student provides an incorrect response, or (f) it is not the appropriate time to be teaching this skill.

(continues)

Figure 5. *(continued)*

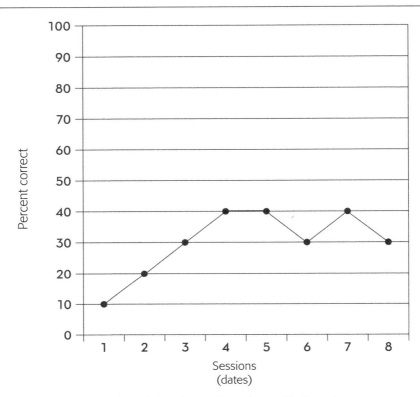

Graph 3. This student did not know the color red before the instructor began teaching this skill. The student began by learning the color red at a steady rate (constant upward slope). After a few sessions the student's learning plateaued (no downward or upward trend), and she has not made any more progress. The instructor needs to reevaluate the teaching procedure and compare the data from the first four sessions to the data from the last four sessions to determine what changed and has impeded the student from progressing further. Once the impediment has been identified, the instructor needs to make appropriate adjustments to the teaching procedure before proceeding. To detect the impediment the instructor could examine (a) a change in instructors, (b) a change in type or level of prompting, (c) a change in type or level of reinforcement, (d) a change in materials used, (e) a change in the environment in which the student is taught, (f) a change in the student's personal life, and (g) an overall change in the student's learning progress across all skills, among other things.

Figure 5. (*continued*)

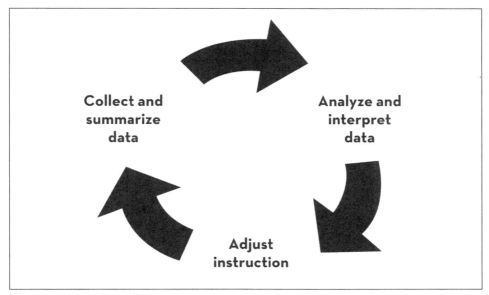

Figure 6. Data-based decision-making process.

The diagram in Figure 6 provides an overview of the cyclical process of using data to assess and plan a student's educational program. Viewing that process as a cyclical routine enables one to understand how a team continually uses data to adjust and improve instruction in order to amend and improve a student's learning and progress.

7 Performance Evaluation of Instructor Implementation of DTT

One of the most important aspects regarding ABA, and thus DTT, is that it is a scientifically based intervention. This means that the method is subjected to the scientific rigors of determining its efficacy through objective and empirical data collection and analysis; that it has specific guidelines for correct or incorrect implementation; and that users need to, and can, determine if the DTT protocol that is being used to teach an individual is being implemented with fidelity (accurately).

In 2000, Cautilli, Rosenwasser, and Clark stated that poorly trained instructors are one of the greatest challenges facing the behavioral sciences. The National Research Council (2001) and the National Professional Development Center on Autism Spectrum Disorders (2010) both identified staff training as a necessary and critical component of high quality educational and behavioral services for children with ASD. Relative to research on DTT, significant work has focused on an instructor's ability to reliably, and with validity, implement DTT in teaching children new skills. While we understand the need to ensure a high level of instructors' fidelity of implementation of DTT, two crucial research-based questions have risen to the top: (a) what are the crucial aspects of DTT that we need to always evaluate and ensure that instructors implement with fidelity?; and (b) what are the best ways to effectively and efficiently train and provide feedback to instructors to ensure a high percentage of fidelity of implementation of DTT? (Babel et al., 2008; Belfiore et al., 2008; Bolton & Mayer, 2008; Crockett, Fleming, Doepke, & Stevens, 2007; Downs, Downs, Johansen, & Fossum, 2007; Gilligan, Luiselli, & Pace, 2007; Leblanc, Ricciardi, & Luiselli, 2005; Severtson & Carr, 2012).

Ensuring *treatment integrity, procedural integrity,* or *fidelity of implementation* with a specific intervention, such as DTT, requires that we evaluate, document, and improve, through specific methods of feedback, the instructor's delivery or use of DTT, as it is defined, on a repeated basis. It is also necessary to make certain that all instructors are consistently teaching each learner using the same DTT methods, thereby ensuring that this scientifically based intervention method is being implemented as designed and, thus, is maximally effective.

Relative to evaluating the overall implementation of DTT, research has demonstrated we not only need to evaluate specific instructional components, but also the *sequence* in which the components are implemented (Babel et al., 2008). Instructors need to be able to generalize their teaching skills across varying environments, children, and skill programs (Bolton & Mayer, 2008). This "how to" manual on DTT describes the various and crucial components of DTT and the methods of delivery, as well as the order in which an instructor uses the strategies and/or implements specific procedures. Methods for training and evaluating new instructors in using DTT, including ways to give instructors effective and corrective feedback, is also outlined.

Research provides us with considerable guidance on effective staff training techniques. In general, the techniques that have been found to be most effective in behavior skills training (BST) are those that include a package of procedures that include, but are not limited to

- reading written explanations (theory),
- watching experts model the techniques,
- role-playing and practicing using the techniques with other adults and then children,
- watching videos of other instructors using the techniques in applied settings, and
- receiving corrective feedback (coaching) on performance from a field-based expert after being observed (Bolton & Mayer, 2008; Leblanc et al., 2005; Schepis, Ownbey, Parsons, & Reid, 2000; Severtson & Carr, 2012).

In sum and most essentially, when ensuring that instructors maintain and generalize the use of their DTT methods, performance feedback is the most effective strategy in fidelity of implementation (Schepis et al., 2000).

Utilizing this manual as the written explanation regarding the theory behind and procedures for implementing DTT will enable potential and neophyte instructors to understand the instructional techniques and sequence of DTT implementation. To be effective and successful in helping potential instructors (trainees) gain the knowledge and skills that are presented in lecture format, trainers should (a) include videos from current and familiar (to the potential instructors) teaching situations and settings in which competent instructors are using DTT techniques with children; (b) provide opportunities for trainees to watch the trainer or other competent instructors model the specific techniques in the same moment that it is being discussed; and (c) provide opportunities for the trainees to practice and role-play using the techniques with one another.

Immediately following this initial training, the trainees/instructors need to be placed in the teaching settings in which they will be working and be observed utilizing specified techniques with the children. The trainer/coach then provides feedback on their performance through specific praise or correction based on their demonstration of the specific skills/behaviors listed on the evaluation forms. These forms (provided in the appendices), used during these observations, determine the new instructors' fidelity of implementation with the DTT techniques. It is important to maintain copies of these evaluation forms so that progress toward competency can continually be reviewed and tracked over time.

As just stated, trainees ideally begin their practice in the teaching setting in which they will be working. Initially, performance evaluation and feedback need to be provided on the overall implementation of the crucial components of DTT. This assists the trainer/coach in identifying the specific areas that need improvement. An evaluation form has been developed and tested regarding this overall implementation of DTT components and has proven to be effective in ensuring instructors' fidelity of implementation of DTT.

The developers of this form (Babel et al., 2008) identified 21 research-based, crucial components of DTT. This DTT evaluation procedure involved (a) having experts in DTT assess the face value of each component, (b) having current practitioners use it to score new instructors implementing DTT, and finally (c) having these same DTT experts watch videos of those new instructors using the form to rate the new instructors and compare the experts' ratings to the practitioners. The resulting evaluation form, *Discrete-Trials Teaching Evaluation Form* (DTTEF), has proven to be effective and reliable in determining instructors' competency with implementing the crucial components of DTT. This form includes what the instructors need to be doing before, during, and after a teaching session. This evaluation is not to be confused with evaluating the components of general session management (as discussed in the section on session management).

The following is a list of the 21 components, cited in the sequence and sections (before, during, and after the DTT session) in which Babel et al. (2008) intended the DTTEF to be used:

☆ Before Starting a Teaching Task

1. Determine teaching task.
2. Gather materials.
3. Select effective reinforcers.
4. Determine prompt-fading procedure and initial fading step.
5. Develop rapport/positive mood.

☆ Manage Antecedents

6. Arrange teaching materials.
7. Secure child's attention.
8. Present teaching materials.
9. Present correct instruction.
10. Present prompts.

☆ Manage Consequences: Correct Response

11. Praise and present additional reinforcer.
12. Record correct response.
13. Have brief inter-trial interval (3–5 seconds).

☆ Manage Consequences: Incorrect Response

14. Block gently, remove materials, look down (2–3 seconds).
15. Record incorrect response.
16. Secure child's attention.
17. Re-present materials.
18. Re-present instruction and prompts to guarantee correct response.
19. Give praise only.
20. Record error correction.
    Repeat #13—Brief inter-trial interval (3–5 seconds)

☆ Across All Trials

21. Fade prompts across trials.

The different procedures discussed previously in this book provide the structured teaching environment that instructors need for DTT implementation and that students need for skill acquisition. Specific performance evaluation forms for these various components are provided in the appendices. Each of these was developed directly from the descriptions provided for that procedure and contains the lists of observable behaviors that new instructors need to demonstrate and on which they need to be evaluated. The performance evaluation forms listed below are provided for use with new DTT instructors and also for periodic maintenance and generalization checks for seasoned practitioners to ensure consistent implementation across time, children, environments, and skill programs.

Appendix B – Evaluation/Observation Form: Reinforcement
Appendix C – Evaluation/Observation Form: Pairing
Appendix D – Evaluation/Observation Form: Instructional Control
Appendix E – Evaluation/Observation Form: Behavioral Momentum
Appendix F – Evaluation/Observation Form: Session Management
Appendix G – Evaluation/Observation Form: Prompting and Fading
Appendix H – Evaluation/Observation Form: Shaping
Appendix K – Evaluation/Observation Form: Token Economy Systems
Appendix L – Evaluation/Observation Form: Discrimination Training

In conclusion, it is important to remember that a dynamic process of training and coaching of DTT skills for potential/new instructors is imperative to the development of instructors who are competent and able to implement DTT with high treatment integrity. Just as each child with ASD is unique and needs individualization of her goals and objectives and the methods by which she is taught, new instructors also need individualization in their training and coaching in order for them to achieve competency. Just as important, objective evaluations are needed in order to learn if potential instructors are unable to achieve competency.

☆ Quick Review: Performance Evaluation of Instructor Implementation of DTT

Training and coaching to develop competent DTT instructors is essential. This process involves providing the trainee with the following:

- lecture training with written explanations and examples;
- video models of competent instructors using techniques;
- opportunities to observe competent instructors modeling use of techniques;
- opportunities to practice and role-play using the new techniques; and
- in-situ observations with a competent trainer/coach using a suitable evaluation form, followed by specific corrective performance feedback.

Fidelity of the above training and coaching will ensure that competency of DTT implementation is achieved, maintained, and generalized across time, settings, children, and skill programs.

8 Conclusion

The DTT instructional method can best be summarized as relying on the foundational S^D–R–S^R elements. These components, as shown in Figure 7, provide an overall picture of how instructors may appropriately view DTT and at which point they will be implementing the various components of DTT as they teach students with ASD. It is important to note that while each of these skills is indicated as occurring at a different point during the DTT process, all of them involve constant adjustment and use throughout a session of teaching.

DTT is a scientifically researched method that has been shown to produce positive results for children and youth with ASD (Dixon et al., 2016; Leaf et al., 2015; Lovaas, 1987; Matson & Jang, 2013; McEachin, Smith, & Lovaas, 1993; NRC, 2001; Smith, 2001). The DTT method provides teachers and others with a structured yet flexible and versatile tool for instruction of students with ASD. An instructor can use it within a 1:1 setting in a home, community, or school environment; within a group setting; and for myriad purposes. ABA, and specifically DTT, will not cure children and youth who have ASD, but it is currently the only comprehensive evidence-based method of teaching them and helping them to acquire the skills and behaviors they need to function appropriately and independently within home, school, and community settings.

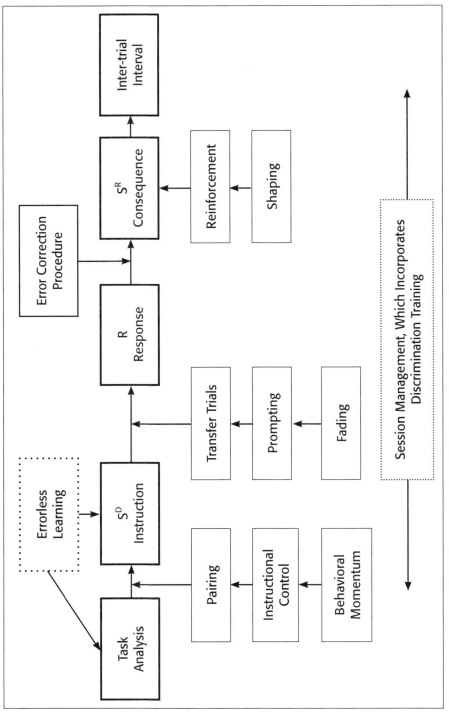

Figure 7. Overview of the discrete trial training (DTT) instructional method.

Task Analysis Checklist

Prior to task analysis of a skill, you need to

- define the target skill/behavior,
- collect data on the current occurrence (or lack) of the behavior—this is called baseline data, and
- write out a clear goal for the student to achieve to demonstrate mastery in learning that skill/behavior.

During task analysis of a skill, you need to analyze the skill you will be teaching by

- determining if the student has the prerequisite skills to learn the new target skill,
- watching someone perform the skill or performing the skill yourself to determine all the smaller sequential components of the skill,
- writing down, in the proper sequence, the steps that occur,
- making any needed adjustments by having someone else follow the exact sequence of steps listed to evaluate the overall analysis and determine if

  - a step has been omitted and
  - the person reaches the same, planned end result, and

- describing and creating (if needed) the materials that will be used when teaching the skill.

After task analysis is completed, you should have a set of steps that are

- discrete (isolated and distinct from each other),
- manageable and logical for the student to perform once he or she has learned the previous step, and
- well described, so that every instructor teaches them the same way and knows what to expect the student to do (S^D, R, and S^R are defined for each step).

Person observed: _____   Date: _____

    + = achieved   − = not achieved   n/a = not able to observe

Goal	Achieved?	Notes
The instructor completes a reinforcement assessment before working with the student.		
Appropriate materials and reinforcers are ready before the session begins.		
If appropriate: The instructor provides the student with the choice of a larger reinforcer to be gained at the end of a *successful* teaching session.		
The instructor maintains student motivation by providing *appropriate* (a smaller amount for lesser demands, etc.) reinforcement.		
The instructor reinforces the student only for correct responses.		
When the instructor provides reinforcement, it is done *immediately* after the correct response.		
The student cannot reach reinforcers or gain reinforcement except through the instructor.		
If using tangible reinforcement, the instructor provides specific praise along with the reinforcer.		
Overall, the session is positive and fun.		

Appendix C
Evaluation/Observation Form: Pairing

Person observed: _____   Date: _____

+ = achieved   − = not achieved   n/a = not able to observe

Goal	Achieved?	Notes
The instructor does not place demands on the student when initially pairing with him or her.		
The instructor offers access to reinforcers in small amounts to increase the frequency of interaction with the student.		
The instructor offers access to reinforcers that the student cannot access independently (can obtain only through the instructor).		
The instructor does not interrupt the student while he or she is engaging in a reinforcing activity (unless it is time to end the activity).		
The student allows the instructor to play next to him or her and occasionally touch or play with the same items.		
The instructor ends the session on a positive response.		
Overall, the session is positive and fun.		

○|○ *Appendix D*
Evaluation/Observation Form: Instructional Control

Person observed: _____   Date: _____

+ = achieved   − = not achieved   n/a = not able to observe

Goal	Achieved?	Notes
The instructor and the student pair successfully, and the student views the instructor as a reinforcer (does not try to run away).		
Initially, the instructor provides reinforcement for every instruction.		
Initially, the instructor provides easy requests (S^Ds) and instructions.		
The instructor provides appropriate amounts of reinforcement to maintain the strength of the reinforcer.		
The instructor maintains control of the reinforcers; access to reinforcement is only through the instructor.		
The instructor avoids presenting S^Ds that compete with any existing reinforcement that is occurring.		
The instructor increases the number and difficulty of tasks gradually over time; more is required of the student for the same amount of reinforcement.		
The instructor ends the session on a positive response.		
Overall, the session is positive and fun.		

Appendix E
Evaluation/Observation Form: Behavioral Momentum

Person observed: _____   Date: _____

+ = achieved   − = not achieved   n/a = not able to observe

Goal	Achieved?	Notes
The instructor follows the 6 components of establishing behavioral momentum: (1) 3–5 easy beginning tasks (2) Small reinforcement for easy tasks (3) Quick pace (4) 3 easy tasks before first difficult task (5) Higher reinforcement for more difficult task (6) Easy and difficult tasks interspersed		
The instructor recognizes when he or she has lost behavioral momentum and can offer a possible explanation as to why.		
The instructor demonstrates using the behavioral momentum strategies to gain momentum back.		
The instructor does not continually demonstrate difficulties with building and maintaining behavioral momentum with the student during the teaching session.		
Overall, the session is fun and positive.		

Evaluation/Observation Form: Session Management

Person observed: _____   Date: _____

   + = achieved   − = not achieved   n/a = not able to observe

Goal	Achieved?	Notes
Appropriate materials and reinforcers are ready before the session begins.		
The student is appropriately positioned and oriented toward the instructor and materials.		
The student is positioned so that distractions in the environment are minimized.		
The instructor maintains a high level of success by mixing easy and more difficult tasks.		
The instructor maintains student motivation by providing appropriate reinforcement.		
The instructor presents a sufficient number of trials per session.		
The instructor ends the session on a positive response.		
Overall, the session is positive and fun.		

Appendix G
Evaluation/Observation Form: Prompting and Fading

Person observed: _____   Date: _____

S^D	Prompt type	Faded? (Y/N—how?)	Response correct? (Y/N)	Notes
1.				
2.				
3.				
4.				

Evaluation/Observation Form: Shaping

Person observed: _____   Date: _____

+ = achieved   − = not achieved   n/a = not able to observe

Identify shaping steps (closer successive approximations):

_____

_____

_____

_____

Goal	Achieved?	Notes
The instructor mixes new S^D/skill with mastered skills.		
The instructor does not require a behavior that has not yet been displayed by the student.		
The instructor reinforces all approximations.		
The instructor provides the highest level of reinforcement for the most independent response.		
The instructor ends the session on the most independent response.		
Overall, the session is positive and fun.		

Evaluation/Observation Form: Error Correction Procedure

Person observed: _____   Date: _____

+ = performed   − = not performed   n/a = not able to observe

Step within procedure	Performed?	Notes
The instructor presents the S^D with the correct answer as a prompt (until the correct response is made by the student).		
The instructor uses the least intrusive prompts.		
The instructor fades prompts appropriately.		
The instructor provides the original un-prompted S^D before proceeding to a distractor trial.		
The instructor presents an easy distractor trial.		
The instructor restates the original S^D after the distractor trial.		
The instructor returns to the original unprompted S^D before the end of the session.		
Overall, the session is positive and fun.		

Token Board

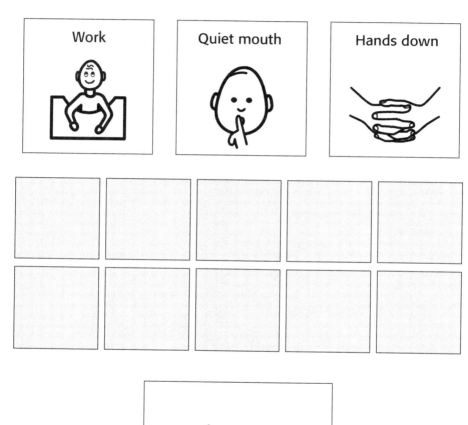

Evaluation/Observation Form: Token Economy Systems

Person observed: _____   Date: _____

  + = achieved   − = not achieved   n/a = not able to observe

Goal	Achieved?	Notes
The instructor uses only 2–3 rules at a time as target-appropriate learning behaviors.		
The instructor uses reinforcement sampling frequently enough to know the highest level reinforcer the student wants.		
The instructor reviews the rules with the student before each teaching session.		
The instructor uses behavioral momentum to start the student earning tokens easily and to maintain student engagement during the session.		
The instructor praises the student using specific language about the rules he or she is following.		
The instructor tells the student when he or she is not following the rules.		
The instructor has the student physically exchange the tokens for the reinforcer.		
The instructor gradually increases the difficulty for earning tokens as the student progresses with learning.		
Overall, the session is positive and fun.		

Evaluation/Observation Form: Discrimination Training

Person observed: _____ Date: _____

  + = achieved   − = not achieved   n/a = not able to observe

Goal	Achieved?	Notes
The instructor demonstrates the mass trial phase appropriately: (1) Isolation stage (2) Distractor stage (3) Block trial stage		
The instructor demonstrates the expanded trial phase appropriately.		
The instructor demonstrates the random rotation phase appropriately.		
The instructor uses transfer trials appropriately during discrimination training.		
The instructor records the correct data based on the phase of teaching.		
The instructor ends the session on the most independent response.		
Overall, the session is positive and fun.		

Procedure Sheets

Waiting Skills

Student: _____

Date introduced: _____

Amended: _____

Mastered: _____

Aim: The aim of this drill is to teach [student name] to wait for access to an item, without snatching the item. For [student name], it is important to future social and play development that he/she be able to be patient in a variety of situations without engaging in inappropriate behavior.

Procedure:
1. When student makes requests for items/activities, practice "waiting" in the following manner:
    a. After a request for an item, use [student name]'s visual to show the expected wait time.
    b. Give the student the visual and deliver the S^D.
    c. Start the timer for the required period.
2. When the student is sitting at the desk while activities are being set up,
    a. While the materials are being arranged on the desk, give the student the visual for "wait" and deliver the S^D.
    b. Start the timer for the required period.
3. If no behaviors (snatching the item, eloping, or touching materials) occur during the waiting period and the student waits appropriately, deliver the requested item/activity.
    a. Take the visual from the student.
    b. Say, "You waited nicely" or "Nice waiting."
    c. Deliver reinforcer; [student name] does not need to repeat the request.
    d. [student name] should be given access to the item only if he/she has waited appropriately.
4. If at any point [student name] engages in inappropriate behaviors,
    a. Take the visual from the student.
    b. Stop the timer.
    c. Remind the student to wait while putting the "wait" visual back in front of him.
    d. Restart the timer.

5. If 2 unsuccessful wait trials occur in succession, for the next trial run an errorless trial.
   a. Decrease the wait period.
   b. Deliver the visual and the S^D.
   c. Prompt the expected response.
6. Conduct wait sessions across the day.
   a. Aim to practice 5 trials per day.

This procedure should not be practiced every time [student name] requests an item. Create plenty of opportunities for requests that do not involve waiting.

Materials: visual of red oval and the word *wait*, timer, token board/picture representation of rules

Mastery criteria: 5/5 × 3 (3 days, 3 different instructors)

Trial by Trial (see explanation in "Types of Data" section)

Error correction: "No," followed by a corrective statement, e.g., "Wait," then represent S^D (see explanation in "Error Correction Procedure" section)
   Do this twice, then move to errorless.

   S^D: "Wait."
   R: [student name] waits patiently for the requested item without requesting again, with hands down/holding the visual.
   R1: 1:1 schedule of reinforcement. Every time he/she waits appropriately, he/she gets the item requested.

Target skill	Intro date	Mastered date	Target skill	Intro date	Mastered date
LEVEL 1:			**LEVEL 3:**		
(a) Waits at desk for preferred item – 10 sec			(a) Waits at desk while instructor leaves – within 1 min, for 1 min		
(b) Waits at desk for preferred item – 20 sec			(b) Waits at desk while instructor leaves – within 2 min, for 1 min		
(c) Waits at desk for preferred item – 30 sec			(c) Waits at desk while instructor leaves – 3 min, within line of sight, for 1 min		
(d) Waits at desk for preferred item – 1 min			(d) Waits at desk while instructor leaves – 3 min, out of sight, 1 min		
LEVEL 2:			**LEVEL 4:**		
(a) Waits at desk for nonpreferred item – 30 sec			(a) Waits at desk while instructor sets up materials – 30 sec		
(b) Waits at desk for nonpreferred item – 1 min			(b) Waits at desk while instructor sets up materials – 1 min		

Receptive Instructions With Visuals

Student: _____

Date introduced: _____

Amended: _____

Mastered: _____

Aim: This drill aims to expand [student name]'s receptive skills and to increase [student name]'s independence in later life. He/she needs to be able to listen to spoken instructions and respond accordingly. The ability to follow receptive instructions will decrease [student name]'s reliance on physical prompting and guidance, therefore increasing his/her independence.

Procedure:
1. Open 2 target skills (see end of Procedure Sheet) at any one time.
2. Intersperse these instructions throughout the day. This may require contriving situations in which to practice the skill (e.g., saying "Get the book" when about to start an activity that needs a book).
3. Ensure the relevant stimuli are available and set up in a field size as indicated in the levels described below (e.g., set up in the playroom a ball, a car, a train, a book, and bubbles for him/her to have to scan and select from).
4. Deliver the S^D.
5. Deliver a functional consequence (e.g., access to food if he/she gets his/her lunchbox).

Items mastered within this drill should be moved to the receptive instructions generalized drill.

Materials: 3D materials, visual prompts (pictures of items to be collected) that are (a) identical to the 3D item and (b) not identical to the 3D item

Mastery criteria: 2×80–100% of opportunities for 2 different therapists

Data collection: Mass Trial – Random Rotation

Error correction:
1. Repeat S^D with prompt. SCORE MINUS/PLUS
2. Use least intrusive prompt possible; continue to repeat step 2 while increasing the prompt until correct response is achieved. SCORE the most EFFECTIVE PROMPT LEVEL.
3. Repeat S^D without prompt. For correct response, move to step 4. For incorrect response, return to step 2.
4. Present VERY easy distractor.

5. Repeat S^D without prompt. If correct, SCORE PLUS or Check. If incorrect, SCORE MINUS or / Slash and return to step 2.
6. Return to S^D after 3–4 other trials.

Prompting:

Most to least

Reduce field size, gesture, or wait time

S^D 1: "Instruction" + hold up visual. (See instructions for target skills below; e.g., "Get book" and hold up picture of a book.)

R1: Student scans area and selects object.

C1: 1:1 schedule of reinforcement. Every time he/she waits appropriately, he/she gets the item requested.

Level 1

(L1a): 5 single-step instructions with identical visual field of 2 items (FO2)

L1a: 10 single-step instructions with identical visual field of 3 items (FO3)

L1b: 10 single-step instructions with NONidentical visual field of 3 items (FO3) (See below for tracking progress with introduction and mastered dates.)

Items/Comments: Intro = Date introduced; Mast = Date mastered (see L1 and L2 above)

Target skill	Intro L1	Mast L1	Intro L1a	Mast L1a	Item	Intro L1	Mast L1	Intro L1a	Mast L1a
Get book					Get bag				
Get biscuit					Put in basket				
Get water					Put in bin				
Get folder					Get lunchbox				
Get the bubbles					Get an iPad				
Get the ball					Get a hat				
Get a puzzle					Get a train				
Get a marker					Get a car				
Get a book					Get playdough				
Get a cup					Get a doll				

Waiting Skills

Trial by trial: 5 trials

Mastery criteria: 5/5 × 3

Error correction: "No," "corrective statement," redeliver S^D × 2, then move to errorless.

Ratio of R+: 1:1

Field size: n/a

S^D: "Wait."

Response (R): "Waits with hands down and quiet mouth for entire time period."

Levels: L1a: 10 seconds; **L1b:** 20 seconds; **L1c:** 30 seconds; **L1d:** 1 minute; etc., L 2, 3, 4 (see Procedure Sheet)

Level								
Date/Therapist								
	+ or −	+ or −	+ or −	+ or −	+ or −	+ or −	+ or −	+ or −
	/5	/5	/5	/5	/5	/5	/5	/5

Receptive Instructions With Visuals

Cold Probe

Mastery criteria: $3 \times 100\%$

Error correction: Repeat S^D with prompt, then repeat S^D without prompt, then easy distractor, then repeat S^D without prompt, return to S^D after 3–4 trials.

Ratio of R+: 1:1 (higher R+ for independent vs. prompt)

Field size: See Procedure Sheet.

Date/Therapist								
	S^D1	S^D1	S^D1	S^D1	S^D1	S^D1	S^D1	S^D1
	Y P N	Y P N	Y P N	Y P N	Y P N	Y P N	Y P N	Y P N
	1 2 3	1 2 3	1 2 3	1 2 3	1 2 3	1 2 3	1 2 3	1 2 3
Date/Therapist								
	S^D1	S^D1	S^D1	S^D1	S^D1	S^D1	S^D1	S^D1
	Y P N	Y P N	Y P N	Y P N	Y P N	Y P N	Y P N	Y P N
	1 2 3	1 2 3	1 2 3	1 2 3	1 2 3	1 2 3	1 2 3	1 2 3
Date/Therapist								
	S^D1	S^D1	S^D1	S^D1	S^D1	S^D1	S^D1	S^D1
	Y P N	Y P N	Y P N	Y P N	Y P N	Y P N	Y P N	Y P N
	1 2 3	1 2 3	1 2 3	1 2 3	1 2 3	1 2 3	1 2 3	1 2 3
Date/Therapist								
	S^D1	S^D1	S^D1	S^D1	S^D1	S^D1	S^D1	S^D1
	Y P N	Y P N	Y P N	Y P N	Y P N	Y P N	Y P N	Y P N
	1 2 3	1 2 3	1 2 3	1 2 3	1 2 3	1 2 3	1 2 3	1 2 3
Date/Therapist								
	S^D1	S^D1	S^D1	S^D1	S^D1	S^D1	S^D1	S^D1
	Y P N	Y P N	Y P N	Y P N	Y P N	Y P N	Y P N	Y P N
	1 2 3	1 2 3	1 2 3	1 2 3	1 2 3	1 2 3	1 2 3	1 2 3

Date/Therapist								
	$S^D 1$	$S^D 1$	$S^D 1$	$S^D 1$	$S^D 1$	$S^D 1$	$S^D 1$	$S^D 1$
	Y P N	Y P N	Y P N	Y P N	Y P N	Y P N	Y P N	Y P N
	1 2 3	1 2 3	1 2 3	1 2 3	1 2 3	1 2 3	1 2 3	1 2 3
Date/Therapist								
	$S^D 1$	$S^D 1$	$S^D 1$	$S^D 1$	$S^D 1$	$S^D 1$	$S^D 1$	$S^D 1$
	Y P N	Y P N	Y P N	Y P N	Y P N	Y P N	Y P N	Y P N
	1 2 3	1 2 3	1 2 3	1 2 3	1 2 3	1 2 3	1 2 3	1 2 3

Cold Probe

Mastery criteria: $3 \times 100\%$

Error correction: Repeat S^D with prompt, then repeat S^D without prompt, then easy distractor, then repeat S^D without prompt, return to S^D after 3–4 trials.

Ratio of R+: 1:1 (higher R+ for independent vs. prompt)

Field size: See Procedure Sheet.

S^D sequence: "Instruction" plus visual

Required response: Gets item.

Levels: See Procedure Sheet.

⦿ Glossary

Antecedent: The stimulus under which a behavior occurs.

Applied behavior analysis: The process of systematically applying the principles of behavior to "improve socially significant behavior to a meaningful degree and to demonstrate experimentally" that the procedures used were actually responsible for the change (improvement) in the behavior (Cooper et al., 1987, p. 14).

Behavior: An action that occurs in response to an antecedent.

Behavioral momentum: Increasing motivation to perform by building up momentum for what the instructor ultimately wants a student to do. This is done by making easy, or "throwaway," demands that the student is likely to think are easy and will thus make the student feel successful. This process makes students more willing to do difficult tasks.

Chaining: Breaking down a complicated skill to be taught to a student into a series of behaviors that occur in a sequence.

Consequence: A response that follows a behavior that will either increase or decrease that behavior.

Discrimination training: Teaching children to distinguish one item (or other response) from another.

Discriminative stimulus (S^D): The instruction, question, or relevant materials presented to the student.

Error correction procedure: A consequence for an incorrect response or failure to respond following the presentation of an S^D.

Errorless learning: Teaching a new skill in a way that minimizes the possibility of errors and thus increases the possibility that the student will be a successful learner.

Fading: The systematic withdrawal of prompts that have been provided to help a learner correctly respond to an S^D.

Instructional control: The instructor's establishment of a high probability of evoking a correct response from a particular student.

Inter-trial interval: The time and space between the occurrences of one trial of S^D–R–S^R and the next trial of S^D–R–S^R.

Pairing: The instructor's linking of himself or herself with items and activities that the student already prefers and thereby establishing himself or herself as a reinforcer.

Prompt: A stimulus, provided along with an S^D, that aids the student in making a correct response. There are two ways of providing prompts:

- least intrusive prompt—the most subtle prompt from which the student will be able to give the correct response; and
- most intrusive prompt—the most obvious prompt from which the student will be able to give the correct response.

Rapid responding: The requirement of a student to respond within 1 second of receiving an S^D; otherwise, the instructor immediately prompts the student to provide the correct response.

Reinforcement: A consequence that follows a student's response and increases the likelihood that the response (behavior) will occur again in the future.

Reinforcer: Something that the student wants to gain (e.g., food, attention, avoidance of difficult tasks).

Session management: Structuring of instruction and work time to maximize opportunities for student learning.

Shaping: Developing a new behavior or skill through reinforcement of closer and closer approximations of the desired behavior.

Strength of reinforcer: The amount of motivation that a reinforcer elicits.

Task analysis: The process of breaking a skill down into individual and sequential teaching steps.

Transfer trial: A method for fading prompts or for providing prompts that are less intrusive than previously applied prompts or learning supports.

References

American Psychiatric Association. (2013). *Diagnostic and statistical manual of mental disorders* (5th ed.). Washington, DC: Author.

Atwood, T. (1998). *Asperger's syndrome: A guide for parents and professionals.* Philadelphia, PA: Kingsley.

Babel, D. A., Martin, G. L., Fazzio, D., Arnal, L., & Thomson, K. (2008). Assessment of the reliability and validity of the discrete-trials teaching evaluation form. *Developmental Disabilities Bulletin 36*(1&2), 67–80.

Belfiore, P. J., Fritts, K. M., & Herman, B. C. (2008). The role of procedural integrity: Using self-monitoring to enhance discrete trial instruction (DTI). *Focus on Autism and Other Developmental Disabilities, 23*(2), 95–102. doi: 10.1177/1088357607311445

Bolton, J., & Mayer, M. D. (2008). Promoting the generalization of paraprofessional discrete trial teaching skills. *Focus on Autism and Other Developmental Disabilities, 23*(2), 103–111. doi: 10.1177/1088357608316269

Burack, J. A., & Volkmar, F. R. (1992). Development of low- and high-functioning autistic children. *Journal of Child Psychology and Psychiatry, 33,* 607–616.

Cautilli, J. D., Rosenwasser, B., & Clarke, K. (2000). Best practices in the administration of behavioral health rehabilitation services (wrap around) in Pennsylvania: Six basic problems and their solutions. *The Behavior Analyst Today, 1*(2), 42–56. Available from: http://www.behavior.org.

Coon, J. T., & Miguel, C. F. (2012). The role of increased exposure to transfer-of-stimulus-control procedures on the acquisition of intraverbal behavior. *Journal of Applied Behavior Analysis, 45,* 657–666. doi: 10.1901/jaba.2012.45-657

Cooper, J. O., Heron, T. E., & Heward, W. L. (1987). *Applied behavior analysis.* Upper Saddle River, NJ: Prentice Hall.

Crockett, J., Fleming, R. K., Doepke, K. J., & Stevens, J. (2007). Parent training: Acquisition and generalization of discrete trials teaching skills with parents of children with autism. *Research in Developmental Disabilities, 28,* 23-36. doi:10.1016/j.ridd.2005.10.003

Dixon, D. R., Linstead, E., Granpeesheh, D., Novack, M. N., French, R., Stevens, E., & Powell, A. (2016). An evaluation of the impact of supervision intensity, supervisor qualifications, and caseload on outcomes in the treatment of autism spectrum disorder. *Behavior Analysis in Practice, 9*(4), 339–348. doi: 10.1007/s40617-016-0132-1

Downs, A., Downs, R. C., Johansen, M., & Fossum, M. (2007). Using discrete trial teaching within a public preschool program to facilitate skill development in students with developmental disabilities. *Education & Treatment of Children, 30*(3), 1–27. http://dx.doi.org/10.1353/etc.2007.0015

Fiske, K. E., Isenhower, R. W., Bamond, M. J., Delmolino, L., Sloman, K. N., & Larue, R. H. (2015). Assessing the value of token reinforcement for individuals with autism. *Journal of Applied Behavior Analysis, 48*(2), 448–453. doi: 10.1002/jaba.207

Gilligan, K. T., Luiselli, J. K., & Pace, G. M. (2007). Training paraprofessional staff to implement discrete trial instruction: Evaluation of a practical performance feedback intervention. *Behavior Therapist, 30,* 63–66.

Green, G. (1996). Evaluating claims about treatments for autism. In C. Maurice, G. Green, & S. C. Luce (Eds.), *Behavioral intervention for young children with autism: A manual for parents and professionals* (pp. 15–43). Austin, TX: PRO-ED.

Hackenberg, T. D. (2009). Token reinforcement: A review and analysis. *Journal of the Experimental Analysis of Behavior, 91*(2), 257–286. doi: 10.1901/jeab.2009.91-257

Knapp, J., & Turnbull, C. (2014). *A complete ABA curriculum for individuals on the autism spectrum with a developmental age of 1–4 years.* Philadelphia, PA: Jessica Kingsley.

Koegel, R. L., Koegel, L. K., Frea, W. D., & Smith, A. E. (1995). Emerging intervention for children with autism: Longitudinal and lifestyles implications. In R. L. Koegel & L. K. Koegel (Eds.), *Teaching children with autism: Strategies for initiating positive interactions and improving learning opportunities* (pp. 1–15). Baltimore, MD: Brookes.

Leaf, J. B., Leaf, R., McEachin, J., Taubman, M., Ala'I-Rosales, S., Ross, R. K., & Weiss, M. J. (2015). Applied behavior analysis is a science and, therefore, progressive. *Journal of Autism and Developmental Disorders, 46*(2), 720–731. doi: 10.1007/s10803-015-2591-6

Leaf, R., & McEachin, J. J. (Eds.). (1999). *A work in progress: Behavior management strategies and a curriculum for intensive behavioral treatment of autism.* New York, NY: DRL Books.

Leblanc, M. P., Ricciardi, J. N., & Luiselli, J. K. (2005). Improving discrete trial instruction by paraprofessional staff through an abbreviated performance feedback intervention. *Education and Treatment of Children, 28*(1), 76–82.

Lovaas, O. I. (1987). Behavioral treatment and normal educational and intellectual functioning in young autistic children. *Journal of Consulting and Clinical Psychology, 55*(1), 3–9.

MacDuff, G. S., Krantz, P. J., & McClannahan, L. E. (2001). Prompts and prompt-fading strategies for people with autism. In C. Maurice, G. Green, & R. M. Foxx (Eds.), *Making a difference: Behavioral intervention for autism* (pp. 37–50). Austin, TX: PRO-ED.

Malott, R. W., & Trojan Suaez, E. T. (2004). *Principles of behavior* (5th ed.). Upper Saddle River, NJ: Prentice Hall.

Matson, J. L., & Jang, J. (2013). The most commonly reported behavior analytic methods in early intensive autism treatments. *Review Journal of Autism and Developmental Disorders, 1*(1), 80–86. doi: 10.1007/s40489-013-0005-2

Mauk, J. E., Reber, M., & Batshaw, M. L. (1997). Autism and other pervasive developmental disorders. In M. L. Batshaw (Ed.), *Children with disabilities* (4th ed.) (pp. 425–447). Baltimore, MD: Brookes.

Maurice, C., Green, G., & Luce, S. C. (Eds.). (1996). *Behavioral intervention for young children with autism: A manual for parents and professionals.* Austin, TX: PRO-ED.

McEachin, J. J., Smith, T., & Lovaas, O. I. (1993). Long-term outcome for children with autism who received early intensive behavioral treatment. *American Journal on Mental Retardation, 97,* 359–372.

McGhan, A. C., & Lerman, D. C. (2013). An assessment of error-correction procedures for learners with autism. *Journal of Applied Behavior Analysis, 46*(3), 626–639. doi: 10.1002/jaba.65

Myles, B. S., & Simpson, R. L. (2003). *Asperger syndrome: A guide for educators and parents* (2nd ed.). Austin, TX: PRO-ED.

National Professional Development Center on Autism Spectrum Disorders. (2010). *Evidence-based practices.* Chapel Hill, NC: Author.

National Research Council, Committee on Educational Interventions for Children with Autism: Division of Behavioral and Social Sciences and Education. (2001). *Educating children with autism.* Washington, DC: National Academy Press.

Partington, J. W. (2006). *The assessment of basic language and learning skills: An assessment, curriculum guide, and skills tracking system for children with autism or other developmental disabilities* (Rev. ed.). Walnut Creek, CA: Partington Behavior Analysts.

Partington, J. W., & Sundberg, M. L. (1998a). *The assessment of basic language and learning skills: An assessment, curriculum guide, and skills tracking system for children with autism or other developmental disabilities.* Danville, CA: Behavior Analysts.

Partington, J. W., & Sundberg, M. L. (1998b). *Teaching language to children with autism or other developmental disabilities* (7th ed.). Danville, CA: Behavior Analysts.

Schepis, M. M., Ownbey, J. B., Parsons, M. B., Reid, D. H. (2000). Training support staff for teaching young children with disabilities in an inclusive preschool setting. *Journal of Positive Behavior Interventions, 2,* 170–178.

Severtson, J. M., & Carr, J. E. (2012). Training novice instructors to implement errorless discrete-trial teaching: A sequential analysis. *Behavior Analysis in Practice, 5*(2), 13.

Simpson, R. L., de Boer-Ott, S. R., Griswold, D. E., Myles, B. S., Byrd, S. E., Ganz, J. E., . . . Adams, L. G. (2004). *Autism spectrum disorders: Interventions and treatments for children and youth.* Thousand Oaks, CA: Corwin Press.

Smith, T. (2001). Discrete trial training in the treatment of autism. *Focus on Autism and Other Developmental Disabilities, 16*(2), 86–92. doi: 10.1177/108835760101600204

Sundberg, M. L. (2008a). *VB-MAPP: Verbal behavior milestones assessment and placement program—A language and social skills assessment program for children with autism or other developmental disabilities* (Guide ed.). Concord, CA: AVB Press.

Sundberg, M. L. (2008b). *VB-MAPP: Verbal behavior milestones assessment and placement program—A language and social skills assessment program for children with autism or other developmental disabilities* (Protocol ed.). Concord, CA: AVB Press.

Taylor, B. A., & McDonough, K. A. (1996). Selecting teaching programs. In C. Maurice, G. Green, & S. C. Luce (Eds.), *Behavioral intervention for young children with autism: A manual for parents and professionals* (pp. 63–177). Austin, TX: PRO-ED.

Van Meter, L., Fein, D., Morris, R., Waterhouse, L., & Allen, D. (1997). Delay versus deviance in autistic social behavior. *Journal of Autism and Developmental Disorders, 27,* 557–569.

Worsdell, A. S., Iwata, B. A., Dozier, C. L., Johnson, A. D., Neibert, P. L., & Thomason, J. L. (2005). Analysis of response repetition as an error-correction strategy during sight-word reading. *Journal of Applied Behavior Analysis, 38,* 511–527. doi: 10.1901/jaba.2005.115-04

About the Editor and Author

About the Editor

Richard L. Simpson was professor emeritus, University of Kansas. During his more than 40 years as a professor of special education at the University of Kansas, he directed numerous demonstration programs for students with autism spectrum disorders (ASD) and other disabilities and coordinated a variety of federal grant programs related to students with ASD and other disabilities. He also worked as a teacher of students with disabilities, a psychologist, and an administrator of programs for students with autism. He was the former editor of the professional journal *Focus on Autism and Other Developmental Disabilities* (published by PRO-ED) and the author of numerous books and articles on ASD.

About the Author

Sonja R. de Boer is a board certified behavior analyst, doctoral level (BCBA-D). She obtained her PhD in special education and psychology and research in education, with an emphasis on autism spectrum disorders (ASD), from the University of Kansas. She has 25 years of experience working in the field of applied behavior analysis (ABA) with students with ASD. In 1994, she was a part of one of the first cohorts (in Sacramento, CA) of ABA therapists trained by the UCLA Institute outside of their center at UCLA. She was also part of one of the first cohorts to become a BCBA in 2000 after the formation of the Behavior Analyst Certification Board (BACB) and its newly established certification process in 1998. Besides the United States, she has worked with ABA professionals, universities, and families with children with ASD in Australia, New Zealand, Ireland, Russia, Nigeria, Chile, Abu Dhabi, and Dubai. She is also the author of *Successful Inclusion Practices for Children with Autism: Creating a Complete, Effective, ASD Inclusion Program* and a coauthor of the book *Autism Spectrum Disorders: Interventions and Treatments for Children and Youth*.